Charles G. Parker

Wagonmaster On The Road To Santa Fe

Charles G. Parker

Wagonmaster On The Road To Santa Fe

Charles R. Strom

Village Press

White City, Kansas

Charles G. Parker: Wagonmaster On The Trial To Santa Fe
©1999 by Charles R. Strom

First Edition
Printed in the United States of America
by The Printery, Junction City, Kansas

Cover Design by Lori Cansler of Redbud DeSigns, White City, Kansas.

Cover background map from THE OLD SANTA FE TRAIL by Stanley
Vestal. Used by permission courtesy of the University of Nebraska Press.
©1939 by Walter Stanley Campbell. ©1967 by Dorothy Callaway and
Mrs. Malory Ausland.

ISBN 0-9671664-0-3

Library of Congress Catalog Card Number: 99-93944

Table of Contents

Introduction

The pursuit of the account of the life of Charles G. Parker has been an exciting yet frustrating experience. Having been raised in the Parkerville community, I have heard stories about this man all of my life. Yet, when hard evidence is sought to substantiate some of the tales that have been accepted in the community as fact, it is discovered that it doesn't seem to exist.

Portions of unknown aspects of his life have had an exciting way of appearing, almost on their own. One such detail pertains to the fact that he had been the proprietor of the Exchange Hotel in Santa Fe. This was totally unknown to this writer until the documents referring to the perjury trial of Francisco Griego were received from Santa Fe. Readers of our earlier local history book, *"That Town Called Parkerville,"* will find some repetition from that work, but will discover a wealth of new material, also. For example, at the time of the completion of that work, I had never heard of the wife named Isabel. Almost by accident, the divorce documents were discovered in the archives of the office of the Clerk of the District Court in Council Grove. I am certain that other information exists that has not been uncovered at this time. Perhaps another edition at a later date will be necessary, if that would be the case.

This book has been constructed in an unorthodox manner simply because of the way that information is available to us. It is a bit like finding a box of photographs of an individual that had been taken throughout the years of that person's life. Suppose that you pour those photos out on a table, and then set about to arrange them to tell that individual's life story. Some of the photos might have other people in them, some might have buildings in the background, others might have far-away scenery in them, but all of them would pertain to the subject of the story. I have used short chapters which might be thought of as a description of those individual photographs, rather than stringing together several unrelated items simply to make the chapters longer.

Instead of using endnotes as many current books of this nature do, I have used footnotes. I personally prefer footnotes because they put the additional information right before you without the irritation of trying to find the correct page at the end of the book. I have used them for two purposes. First, they give references for primary sources, and second, they carry additional information that adds to the text. The reader may ignore the footnotes entirely or may read them as they move along through the text. It is their choice.

Many individuals have been most helpful in providing bits of information that have gone into creating this picture of a true American pioneer. I have given credit to these persons by way of a footnote at the place where this information is used. In addition to individuals, the personnel at the Research Center of the Kansas State Historical Society in Topeka have been of much help. Likewise, the New Mexico Commission of Public Records, State Records Center and Archives, in Santa Fe, and the Missouri Historical Society in St. Louis have added a wealth of information to the overall picture. Last, but not least, the ladies in the office of the Register of Deeds and the Clerk of the District Court in Council Grove have been most helpful in my searches conducted there. And, finally, without the help and encouragement of my wife, Kay, the task would have been impossible.

Charles R. Strom

Parkerville, Kansas
Along the Neosho River
The summer of 1999

Chapter 1
In Retrospect

A casual motorist driving into the little village of Parkerville, in Morris County, Kansas, might never even notice the cemetery on the west edge of the town. It has no great stone wall enclosure nor large archway entrance. A simple wire mesh fence with an open gate gives all the protection that is needed in this out-of-the-way corner of America. There are no great monuments to be found anywhere in this grave yard. Several dozen simple granite and marble markers serve that purpose, and many depressions in the sod indicate the presence of unmarked graves. In fact, this little burying place looks no different than hundreds of others all across rural America.

But if that casual traveler were to spend a few days in research of local history, he would discover that this little cemetery contains the remains of those of a pioneer community unlike most others in middle America.

For example, along the east side stands a small marble shaft, only about two feet high, with the name "R. Stivers" engraved on it.[1] Randal Stivers had arrived in the valley of the Neosho River in about 1869, even before the town was founded. Not only did he carry the usual line of merchandise in his general store, "R. Stivers & Co.," but he also sold agricultural implements and bought and sold grain. This pioneer merchant's life was cut short, when at the age of 53, he died

---

[1] - Randal Stivers was born in Meggs County, Ohio, in 1826. He was one of that great multitude of Americans who moved west looking for a better life. Following his death, his wife, Harriet, began to put the feminine touch on the business with this advertisement that appeared in the April 22, 1880, issue of the Morris County Enterprise, printed in Parkerville, KS - "Prints of the latest styles at H. Stivers." The old firm had a new name, also. The Stivers had no children, but she soon was joined by a nephew, twenty year old Alva Newton Dilley. A few years later he became owner of the store and brought it to new heights of success. He lived out the rest of his life in Morris County, Kansas, and when he died in 1937, his obituary, printed in the December 4th edition of the Council Grove (KS) Republican gave additional insight into the scope of this business when it said, "Frequently a line of wagons nearly a mile long would be waiting to unload wheat at the Dilley warehouse or directly into MK&T freight cars."

of peritonitis. His wife, Harriet took over the business and was the first lady storekeeper in town.

Along the north side of the cemetery is found a plot with several graves in it, containing the family of Samuel Sanford.[1] Sam came to Parkerville from England at the age of seventeen. By the time he was twenty four, the local paper was carrying advertisements of wagons that he had built in his shop. He went on to be involved in many ventures ranging from undertaking to a barbed wire factory.[2] He was without doubt very prosperous and when the town voted bonds to build a city hall, Sam could see his taxes going sky high. He brought suit against the city to halt the sale of the bonds, but he lost. That fact, plus perhaps others, caused him to lose his enthusiasm for Parkerville. He moved to Fayetteville, Arkansas, and there engaged in wagon manufacturing. When he died in 1927, his remains were brought back to the Parkerville cemetery where he was buried beside his wife who had died in 1916, and among the graves of five small children who had all died before they left Parkerville thirty years earlier.

Moving back toward the center of the cemetery, a large granite marker carries the name of James A. Hopkins, MD.[3] He died at age 33, gunned down by the mayor of the town, H. S. Day.[4] Court

[1] - Morris County Enterprise, Parkerville, Morris County, KS - May 10, 1883

[2] - Sam Sanford involved himself in an amazing range of business enterprises in his years in Parkerville. He had a farming operation in addition to making harrows, selling sod-breaking plows, and being a partner in a construction firm. This construction firm, Sanford, Hall & Co., also advertised that they "have the finest lot of coffins ever brought to our city. They also have a very fine assortment of burial robes of all sizes." (Morris County Enterprise, June 5, 1879)

[3] - Dr. James Hopkins was born in Warren County, Kentucky, in 1854, but had moved to Lawrence, Kansas, with his parents the following year. At age eighteen, he began his medical studies in Kansas City. After graduation, he practiced medicine for about a year in Leavenworth County before coming to Parkerville. (Council Grove Republican - October 28, 1887)

[4] - Handy S. Day was another of the movers and shakers in this early community. Local newspaper advertisements prior to the tragedy indicate that he was involved in real estate, insurance, selling nursery stock, operating a steam-driven threshing machine, in addition to conducting tours for prospective emigrants. He was a Civil War veteran and had come to Parkerville from Ohio. He had served as Justice of the Peace and Police Judge (A. T. Andreas - "History of The State of Kansas"

records are quite vague and newspaper accounts are even more so, but it was a family feud of sorts as Dr. Hopkins was married to Mrs. Day's neice. The courts moved swiftly in those days and in less than two months H. S. Day was on his way to prison, found guilty of manslaughter in the second degree. A year and a month later, he was a free man.

A small marker along the west side of the cemetery carries the simple engraved word, "Poole." Here lie the four young children of Mr. and Mrs. Thomas Poole, ranging in age from four to eleven. They were drowned a few miles north of town in a terrible accident. Their teenage brother was bringing them home from school in a wagon pulled by a team of horses. While fording a rain swollen creek, the wagon was hit by a three foot high wall of water. This turned the wagon over, drowning the horses and throwing the children into the raging torrent. The older boy survived but the other children were lost in the flooded creek.[1]

Our casual traveler might find many other interesting tales memorialized by the stones in this little cemetery, but one in particular would stand out. The stone itself is quite common, red in color, and perhaps a bit larger than many, but it is the name on the stone that would catch our eye and our imagination. It is the grave of Charles G. Parker and his second wife, Mattie. This is the last resting place for a true American pioneer.

Chicago, 1883, page 808) At the time of the shooting, he was mayor of Parkerville.

[1] - Morris County Enterprise, November 13, 1879. Mrs. Frank Prescott, writing of her early day remembrances of Ohio Township in the Council Grove Republican of July 21, 1954, gave these additional details - "Neighbors were kind. The children were prepared for burial. A wagon-maker in Parkerville made two caskets. The neighbors lined them the best they could, and placed two girls in one and the other girl and boy in the other." The children were initially buried in a nearby rural school yard but later moved to the Parkerville cemetery where their parents were later buried with them.

The grave marker for Charles G. Parker and his second wife, Mattie Fall Parker, in the town cemetery at Parkerville, Morris County, Kansas.
(Author's Collection)

Chapter 2
America On The Move

The great westward movement in America in 1849 is beyond our imagination. It was brought about almost by accident during normal activities in the Sacramento Valley in California the previous year. John A. Sutter had arrived in the area in 1839. At that time, the territory was still under Mexican rule, so he applied for Mexican citizenship and in the process received land grants of about 50,000 acres. He set about building an adobe fort for protection for the other settlers in the region. In a short time it became an inn, granary, warehouse, and retail store, as well as a fort. Soon the area had a white population of about 300, as well as quite a number of Indians.

About 45 miles from the fort, a sawmill was being constructed. The millrace, the channel for the water being diverted to the water wheel, proved too shallow to provide necessary power to turn the wheel. Work was begun to deepen the millrace, and as John Marshall, the construction superintendent, recalled later, "My eye was caught by something shining in the bottom of the ditch. I reached down and picked it up. It made my heart thump, for I was certain it was gold. The piece was about half the size and shape of a pea."[1]

The reports of the gold find were slow to reach the eastern part of the nation, taking most of the rest of 1848, but once they did, it set off a national fever unparalleled in our history. Companies were formed to ship supplies around Cape Horn. Others carried gold seekers to the Isthmus of Panama for a dangerous trek through the jungle to the other side where other ships awaited them. Most of those bound for the gold fields, however, took one of two overland routes.

Most favored of these two options was the much publicized California-Oregon Trail, which had been in use since 1841, taking settlers to "the Promised Land" of these two states. The greatest problem with this route was the crossing of the mountains in the west.

---

[1] -J. S. Holliday, "The World Rushed In" (New York: Simon & Schuster, 1983), p. 32

The other choice was the Santa Fe Trail. While the mountains created no great challenge on this route, lack of water in some areas and hostile Indians in others created their own special hazards. This trail followed a southwesterly track into the territory of New Mexico, newly acquired by conquest in 1846. For the gold seekers, there were several branches of the trail from Santa Fe, all heading west into southern California. To those people who watched their neighbors sell everything they had to make the trek to California, it must have seemed like all of America would be on the west coast in another year. While that great migration was taking place, though, other Americans were on the move to other places.

Charles G. Parker was also headed west, first passing through Council Grove, Kansas, in 1849, on his way to Santa Fe. He was not headed to California, though. He was with a government wagon train taking supplies to the U.S. Army in New Mexico Territory.[1]

Council Grove is located on the Neosho River in the Flint Hills of Eastern Kansas. It's history is dramatically intertwined with the history of the Santa Fe Trail. Council Grove is thought to have been named by George Sibley, who at that place entered into a treaty with the Osage Indians on August 10, 1825, for the right to survey the Santa Fe Trail through their territory. In return they were awarded $800 worth of merchandise.[2] Council Grove, a hundred and forty-five miles west of Independence, MO., was on the western edge of "civilization." It was here that for safety, smaller groups of wagons were bunched together into the great caravans that moved across the prairie. Stanley Vestal says "Council Grove, the point at which caravans organized for their long cruise to the Mexican settlements, was one of the most agreeable stopping-places on the Trail. It consisted of a continuous strip of timber nearly half a mile wide, extending along the valley of a small, running stream known as Council Grove Creek, the principal branch of the Neosho River. Along this stream were fertile bottoms and beautiful upland prairies. The Grove itself contained many fine old trees; ash, oak, elm, maple,

---

[1] - A. T. Andreas, -"History of The State of Kansas", Chicago, 1883,   pg. 808
[2] - Gregory Franzwa, "The Santa Fe Trail Revisited" Patrice Press, St. Louis 1989, pg. 72

and hickory, festooned with enormous grapevines, and it covered altogether about one hundred and sixty acres."[1]

One of the many unanswered questions about Charles G. Parker is "How did he happen to settle in the valley at the point that he did?" The farm that he bought later in life was about twelve miles up the Neosho valley northwest of Council Grove. A possible answer could be that during one of his stays at the rendezvous point at Council Grove, he roamed up the valley and found a spot that he liked. Perhaps he said to himself, "Someday when I retire from the Trail, this is where I want to live." That's pure speculation, of course, but very possible.

The timber growing along the Neosho River provided the last opportunity to acquire hardwoods for wagon repairs for the trip. Josiah Gregg described this aspect of the stop on the Neosho in these words - "During our delay at the Council Grove the laborers were employed in procuring timber for axle-trees and other wagon repairs, of which a supply is always laid in before leaving this region of substantial growths; for henceforward there is no wood on the route fit for these purposes; not even in the mountains of Santa Fe do we meet with any serviceable timber. The supply procured here is generally lashed under the wagons, in which way a log is not infrequently carried to Santa Fe, and even sometimes back again."[2]

When Parker made that first trip through Council Grove in 1849 there were only four log houses in the town.[3] Before many years had passed, though, the trail traffic had increased to almost unbelievable proportions. The Kansas Press, printed in Cottonwood Falls, KS, at that time, but later moving to Council Grove, carried this very interesting report on the Santa Fe trade-

"SANTA FE TRADE - We are indebted to S. M. Hays and Co., of Council Grove, for a statement of the trade upon the Santa Fe road. This does not include the Pike's Peak emigration, but is the legitimate trade of the road. From this statement, it appears that in a little over one month, there were engaged in this trade, 647 men, 418 wagons, 164 horses, 1878 mules, 5,622 oxen, 14 carriages, --that they

---

[1] - Stanley Vestal, "The Old Santa Fe Trail", Lincoln, NE, 1939, pg. 55

[2] - Josiah Gregg, "Commerce of the Prairies," Chicago, 1926, pg. 37

[3] - A. T. Andreas, -"History of The State of Kansas", Chicago, 1883, pg. 808

transported over the plains one thousand and seventy tons of freight, besides 1,600 sheep."[1]

The freight through Council Grove continued to increase with the passing of time. By 1866, the local editor made this observation - "For a week past, there has been one continual throng of wagons passing, to and fro, on Santa Fe Avenue. Even the devil himself couldn't keep count and attend to his legitimate business. Several large trains, eastward bound, are encamped out west of town, and as we put this in type, the main thoroughfare is completely lined with large caravans heavily loaded, from Kansas City, as far as the eye can reach, east and west."[2]

The W. F. Shamleffer and C. N. James store on
Main Street in Council Grove on the Santa Fe Trail.
(*Courtesy Kansas State Historical Society*)

---

[1] - "Kansas Press"- Cottonwood Falls, KS June 13, 1859
[2] - "Council Grove Democrat"- June 1, 1866

8

Chapter 3
On The Trail To Santa Fe

Efforts to gather information about a subject are always hampered by the passage of time, but in researching the life of Charles G. Parker, special problems continued to crop up. An example of this pertains to his date of birth. He may have been born in Mansfield, Windom County, CT, on May 5, 1820,[1] or in Manchester County, CT, on May 9, 1820.[2] Or perhaps he was actually born on May 5, 1821, as is recorded on his grave marker in the Parkerville cemetery.

The best efforts of the Connecticut Historical Society and the services of a professional genealogist in that area have failed to produce any solid evidence about his parents. It is known that a Charles and Anna Parker lived in that area and that a child was born to them in 1817. This may have been a brother, Henry S. Parker, who was living in St. Louis in 1870. He played an important role in his brother Charley's life in later years.

According to his obituary, Charles was orphaned at age ten, so, he said "he pushed his own way through life."[3] He had five brothers and three sisters, "All of whom preceded him to the other world several years ago."[4] One can only imagine what may have transpired in those first twenty-nine years of his life. It is possible that he had other older siblings in St. Louis, and that he had gone there to live with them. We might imagine him, as a young child, watching the river boats moving up the Missouri River headed to Westport, and saying to himself, "Someday I'll see Santa Fe for myself." We can only speculate about his early years, but we know that he felt the same draw to go west that so many others were experiencing in that period of American history.

After that first notice of Parker passing through Council Grove in 1849 with the government wagon train, he disappears from

---

[1] - Obituary - Council Grove Guard - September 17, 1909
[2] - A. T. Andreas, -"History Of The State Of Kansas", Chicago, 1883, pg. 808
[3] - Obituary - Council Grove Guard - September 17, 1909
[4] - Ibid.

view for several years. Those years probably included several trips to Santa Fe, but the first one would have been the one that Parker would have remembered all of his life.

Life in New Mexico in the mid nineteenth century was much different than that of pioneer America. Nearly every writer that has recorded their impressions of their first trip across the plains indicates a similar culture shock as they approached their destination. Eighteen year old Susan Magoffin expressed this kind of surprise on her first trip to the southwest. Married less than eight months to Samuel Magoffin, 45 years old and a veteran of Santa Fe trade, she saw sights that she could hardly believe. Her diary reveals the shock of a culture much different than that of her proper Kentucky upbringing.

"The women slap about with their arms and necks bare, perhaps their bosoms exposed (and they are not the prettiest or whitest). If they are about to cross the little creek that is near all the villages, regardless of those about them, they pull their dresses which in the first place but little more than cover their calves—up above their knees and paddle through the water like ducks, sloshing and spattering every thing about them.

"And it is repulsive to see the children running about perfectly naked, or if they have on a chimese (sic), it is in such ribbands (sic) it had better be off at once. I am constrained to keep my veil drawn closely over my face all the time to protect my blushes."[1]

First time travelers were also amazed at the confusion and activity in this strange foreign city at the end of the trail. Marian Russell described it like this, "We moved along narrow alley-like streets past iron-barred windows. We were among a scattering of low, square-cornered adobe houses. We saw a church with two cupolas. Mexicans, Indians, and half-breeds shouldered by us. We saw strings of red peppers drying, and brown babies asleep by old adobe walls.

"Our caravan wriggled through donkeys, goats and Mexican chickens. We came to the plaza and found there a man, a tall man, leaning on a long rifle. He had a long neck like a turkey, red and

---

[1] -Susan Shelby Magoffin - "Down The Santa Fe Trail And Into Mexico" New Haven 1926, pg. 95.

wrinkled, but he was boss of the plaza. We went where he told us. Under his guidance, wagon after wagon fell into place. Dogs barked at us. Big-eyed children stared at us. Black-shawled women smiled shyly at us. We were in Santa Fe."[1]

What a pity that twenty-nine-year-old Charles Parker failed to record his impressions of his first trip across the plains. He might have given us a different slant on the strange sights to be seen in this foreign city at the end of the trail. If it is safe to conclude that he had spent some of his earlier years in St. Louis, he would have been familiar with the mid-nineteenth century big city, but he had never seen anything like this one just before him. Two themes recur in most of the first-hand tales of Santa Fe - the unusual appearance of the city and the morality (or perceived lack thereof) of the inhabitants.

William Brown brings these two themes into focus for us. "From a distance the town looked like a great brickyard—flat-roofed, one-story adobe houses it's kilns. It's most imposing building, the Governors' Palace was, as one writer describes it, but a straggle of mud. The plaza, heart of the town and its marketplace, was dirt and confusion shaded by a few ragged cottonwoods, mules and wagons and men thronging the center, where lank Missourians stopped short at strange sounds and sights—Indians from nearby pueblos, rebozo-wrapped Spanish matriarchs trudging purposefully to church, dried meat and chiles hanging from surrounding portals, funeral processions, ragged children dashing by, and, most intriguing, the young women with their glaring escorts.

"In Santa Fe was found a different morality that shocked or pleased the Americans. Women smoked and often were openly flirtatious. Gambling flourished. Religion was medieval. Ignorance was profound. Yet, sinful, unenlightened, and tyrannized as they were, the people were happy. Once the patronizing American dropped his rigid attitudes, he discovered grace, courtesy, generosity, honesty—perhaps in dishonesty itself—and even an ancient dignity in the people of Santa Fe. Someone young and flexible, like Lewis H. Garrard, found biblical charm in women drawing water from a community well. A mature, long-term resident like James Josiah

---

[1] -Marian Russell, "Land of Enchantment, Memoirs of Marian Russell along the Santa Fe Train" - Albuquerque, 1981, pg. 29

Webb found decorum and much to be admired in the traditional society. A rigid Victorian like W. W. H. Davis found little but shocking immorality and with missionary fervor conceived America's duty to be the "improvement" of this misguided race. Santa Fe was many things to those who saw it."[1]

Though we can never know his exact thoughts about Santa Fe, we do know that Charles Parker chose to be associated with the trail and with the city for nearly twenty years.

Santa Fe, as it would have looked to those early travelers.
(Courtesy Museum of New Mexico Negative #10205)

---

[1] - William E. Brown - "The Santa Fe Trail" - St. Louis, 1988 - pg. 164

Chapter 4
Trouble On The Trail

Preston Beck, Jr. and James L. Johnson, well-to-do Santa Fe merchants, had discovered that they could enhance their profits if they operated their own wagon train to bring merchandise from "The States." Thirty-six year old Charles G. Parker was signed on as wagon-master, or as once mentioned in the claim documents later filed with the government, "the conductor of the train."

An event took place on one trip that was probably not all that uncommon, but it was of such a nature that caused it to be filed away for more than a century in government documents.[1] The train had progressed more than 350 miles from when it had left the Independence, MO, area to a spot west of modern Dodge City near Fort Atkinson. Because of the damage inflicted on the train by the Indians, a claim was filed with the federal government. Testimony given by Charles G. Parker was recorded as follows—

"Territory of New Mexico,
     County of Santa Fe"

"On this 28th day of August, A. D. 1857, personally came before me, Augustus De Marle, clerk of the United States District Court for the First Judicial District, for the Territory aforesaid, Charles G. Parker, and upon his oath declared that in the month of May, June, and July, 1857, he was wagon-master for the merchant train of Preston Beck, Jr., and James L. Johnson, merchants, trading in New Mexico under the style and firm of 'Beck & Johnson,' transporting goods from Kansas City, Missouri, to Santa Fe, New Mexico; that while on the Arkansas river, near the site of Fort Atkinson, that a large band of Kiowa Indians, 200, more or less, in number, came to the train and assuming a menacing attitude, with arrows drawn and bows strung, ordering me to stop the train and give them blankets, coats, and whatever else they wanted, or they would shoot us through. Some of the drivers became intimidated. I told

---

[1] - My special thanks to Mark Gardner for calling my attention to the 37th Congress, 2nd Session, House of Representatives, Report C. C. No. 290, referred to as Serial Set #1146

13

them if they did not immediately leave we should defend ourselves, and began to get out our guns to do so. The Indians had then followed us some six or eight miles, when their chief (known by the name of 'Peshamo') came to us and told Mr. Preston Beck, Jr., and myself, that we did right in driving the Indians away, but that if we would give to a large number of women and children of his people, who were present, some provisions, he would not permit his people to molest us any more. We gave to them one sack of flour, one sack of crackers, fifty pounds of sugar, fifty pounds of coffee, fifty pounds of rice, one box of smoking tobacco, and some butcher knives. The Indians then all left us, and said they were going to their own camp, but the train had proceeded but a few miles further when two of the same Indians fired their arrows from an ambuscade and killed two mules in the team of the leading wagon of the train, and being on horseback, made their escape at full speed.

"The value of the property given to the Indians to avoid bloodshed and prevent further molestation was not less than one hundred dollars. The mules were of the largest size, and, at that place and under the circumstances, worth not less than $225 each, making the whole amount of loss not less than five hundred and fifty dollars, ($550), not including property taken from the teamsters and otherwise stolen from the train."

Mr. Preston Beck, Jr., in his statement, added this note to the story - "The Arapaho Indians afterwards informed their agent, and a Mr. Allison, that the same chief, 'Peshamo,' had stated to them that the Kiowas had killed the mules to induce the whites *from fear* to give them more sugar and coffee next time."

Additional testimony by Nesario Garay revealed that he was the driver of the foremost team "when two Indians rushed out from an ambuscade and, with arrows, killed two of the largest and fattest mules of the team, and immediately fled on horseback."

Other testimony was given by Francisco Griego, another teamster with the train. He adds very little detail to what had already been said, "Deponent was threatened in the same manner (as the others) and upon refusing to give up anything was punched in the side by an arrow, and would probably have been hurt, had he not been rescued by a Mexican captain (?) among the Indians. The Indians were proceeding further to rifle the wagons, when the men were ordered to take their arms and defend themselves."

The claim by Beck & Johnson against the federal government for damages caused by the Indians would not be paid quickly, and Preston Beck, Jr., would not live to see it happen.

Chapter 5
A Violent Heritage

Santa Fe has a violent history that carried over well into the mid-nineteenth century. Historians tell us that the Spaniard Cabeza de Vaca was the first white man to visit the area. He crossed the present state in 1536, going all the way to the Gulf of California. When he returned to the southern Spanish settlements, he told of rich cities that he had heard about from the Indians. Marcos de Niza set out to look for these cities in 1539, but was unsuccessful in his search. Coronado followed the next year, but no gold was to be found by him, either. However, he did lay claim to the area for Spain.

An effort was made to establish a permanent settlement in the Santa Fe area in 1598, but it failed. Santa Fe was finally founded in 1609 and became the capital of the province. Great efforts were made by the Franciscan monks to "christianize" the Pueblo Indians. They resisted the rigid rules laid upon them, and finally burned Santa Fe in 1680. Twelve years passed before the Spanish returned to reclaim the territory and to re-establish their authority in the area.

In 1821, the same year that William Becknell made his famous journey from Missouri to Santa Fe, the province came under Mexican rule. Peace was short-lived in the area, though, as a border dispute between the US and Mexico flared up into full-fledged war.

"Mexico has passed the boundary of the United States, has invaded our territory and shed American blood upon American soil. War exists, and, notwithstanding all our efforts to avoid it, exists by the act of Mexico herself." So President James K. Polk said in his message to Congress in May of 1846.[1]

It was during this conflict that General Stephen W. Kearny seized the province of New Mexico for the United States. Civil government was quickly set by General Kearny, who appointed

---

[1] - This is an extreme oversimplification of a complex conflict. Other issues complicated the whole affair. President Polk wished to acquire the vast region of California during his presidency. He had tried to purchase it from Mexico, but they refused to sell. Anti-slavery New England opposed the war, fearing it would add more territory for the expansion of slavery.

Charles Bent governor of the new territory on September 22, 1846, along with other necessary officials. Bent, in turn, appointed local officials such as district attorneys, justices of the peace and sheriffs. A semblance of civilization began to exhibit itself. A saw mill was established, troops were drilled daily and even a printing press, brought in from Missouri, was soon in operation,[1]

These were the circumstances as they appeared on the surface of the territory, but there was an undercurrent of rebellion which burst forth on January 19, 1847, with the Taos massacre which resulted in the death of Governor Bent.[2]

With this as its history, Santa Fe was probably somewhat hardened to violence and death. Yet, when the news went out that there was a knife fight in the street and one man was dead and another man, a prominent merchant of the city, was gravely wounded, it must have been a tremendous shock to all who heard it. Here is how the Santa Fe Weekly Gazette carried the news of the tragedy—

"Just as we were finishing an editorial article published in another column under the caption of 'District Court,' a gentleman stepped into our office and asked if we had heard the news. We replied in the negative when he informed us that Mr. Preston Beck, Jr., of the firm of Beck & Johnson, had killed Mr. John Gorman, a clerk in the store of Mr. Richard Owens, in a street fight, and was dangerously wounded himself. We instantly dropped our pen and went up to the plaza to learn the particulars, which are as follows, as we were informed by a highly reliable gentleman who witnessed the scene.

"Francisco Griego,[3] a quiet, steady and faithful peon boy in the employ of Messrs. Beck and Johnson, was passing the store of Mr. Owens, Thursday night, when Mr. Gorman familiarly called him

---

[1] - Ralph Emerson Twitchell, "Old Santa Fe", Chicago, 1925, pg. 286

[2] - Ibid. pg. 288. This period in the history of New Mexico was a time of intrigue and treachery. More detail than has been presented would not be appropriate for this work, but the above-cited reference would be most interesting to the serious student of history

[3] - This is obviously the same Francisco Griego who was a driver of one of the teams in the train of Beck & Johnson when it was attacked by the Kiowa Indians on the Kansas plains the previous year. See chapter 4.

in. After he had gotten in, he asked Francisco if he had taken his (G's,) woman (Francisco's wife's sister,) to a *beile* (ball) on two occasions. Francisco answered in the affirmative. He was then asked if he had not taken her there at another time. Francisco, seeming to be thinking for a moment, did not instantly reply, whereupon Gorman struck him with a stick, and continued beating him until his arms and head and face were a gore of blood. He then opened the door and threw him out into the street, where he was found during the night and taken home. He is now lying dangerously ill, with but slim hopes of recovery.

"On Friday morning Mr. Beck was informed of the outrage perpetrated upon Francisco, (who for a number of years had been his faithful employee) and heard his sworn statement. He then proceeded to the store of Mr. Owens to see Mr. Gorman. He charged him with the outrage. G. denied it and told B. to prove it. Mr. Beck instantly denounced him and the act, in severe terms. Angry words ensued, and Gorman approached Beck with a drawn knife, threatening to serve him as his servant had been served. Mr. Beck (who was standing on the outside of the front door of the store) drew a knife, also. Each commenced parrying the motions of the other, when Gorman made a sudden stroke, thrusting his knife into Mr. Beck's abdomen near the navel. As quick as thought, the lick was returned, Mr. Beck's knife penetrating to the hilt the left side of Gorman, in the region of the heart. Mr. Gorman made several other licks which were skillfully warded off by Mr. Beck, without hitting Gorman, when the latter fell upon his back, his arms outstretched, turned over once, and expired."[1]

Editor Samuel Yost went on to describe the efforts made to save the life of Preston Beck, telling of the sufferings that he endured and that he was encouraged to arrange his business affairs in that his life might be short. He then detailed the effect on the city in these words -

"We have never seen any community so intensely concerned - indeed, almost dumb struck - as were the citizens of Santa Fe on Friday. During the whole day men swarmed the streets, awaiting with

---

[1] -Santa Fe Weekly Gazette, March 27, 1858 - Courtesy the New Mexico Persons Collections, New Mexico State Records Center & Archives, Santa Fe, NM

beating hearts and trembling fear the result of each moment's delay in the reception of information concerning Mr. Beck's life.

"Mr. Beck's correct business habits, courteous and high-toned bearing, and manly and generous qualities of head and heart, have won for him an esteem and confidence rarely enjoyed by any man. In addition to this, his extensive mercantile engagements, ramified throughout the entire Territory, render the bare idea of his loss, so serious a derangement to the various interests of our business people that it is involuntarily shrunk from, with a sense akin to horror."[1]

In spite of all the prayers and concerns of the people who knew him, the life of Preston Beck, Jr. was not to be spared. After lingering for nearly two weeks, he died at about noon on April 7, 1858. The editorial style of the day was quite flowery, but Editor Yost probably captured the somber mood of the city when he wrote - "Hundreds upon hundreds of the native population....men, women and children....crowded the house to get a parting glance at the inanimate clay which so shortly before contained so big a soul. Men, wrapped in their coarse blankets, and to whose harden cheeks, tears....those silent messengers of sorrow....were strangers, felt that a friend, true and tried, had gone, and profusely wept. His own associates trembled and shook with grief, and those who were estranged from him by political association, could not withhold "the passing tribute of a sigh," that he who had ever proved himself the soul of honor, too proud to be mean or selfish, had been called from the conflicts of earthly life to another and we trust a happier state of existence."[2]

The funeral was scheduled for the next day. Before the service, a large crowd assembled at the Court House where a number

---

[1] - Ralph Emerson Twitchell makes this comment - "Several notable affrays and killings took place in Santa Fe, either in or near the old Fonda, or on the plaza; among others the duel with bowie-knives between Preston Beck, a prominent merchant of Santa Fe and John Gorman, in 1858, in which both were killed; the killing of Chief Justice John P. Slough by Col. William L. Rynerson; and the killing of one of the architects of the Catholic cathedral by John B. Lamy, a nephew of the archbishop; all three of which were most lamentable tragedies." Ralph Emerson Twitchell. "Old Santa Fe", Chicago. 1925, pg. 357.

[2] -Santa Fe Weekly Gazette, April 10, 1858 - Courtesy The New Mexico Persons Collections, New Mexico State Records Center & Archives, Santa Fe, NM

of resolutions of respect were passed, being presented both in English and Spanish. After this gathering had concluded their business, they followed the body to it's final resting place. Flags were flown at half-mast, and there was a general suspension of business in the city.[1]

Preston Beck, Jr., was born in Indiana, but moved to Missouri as an infant, where he grew to manhood. He had come to New Mexico in 1845 as a trader and remained there until his death. He had been most successful, gathering considerable wealth in the process. He was about 38 years old and had never married.[2]

We cannot be certain that Charles G. Parker was in Santa Fe at the time of Preston Beck's death, but we know for sure that they were well acquainted with each other. Parker had been in Beck's employment at the time of the Indian attack the previous summer. They had faced danger and even death as fellow-travelers on the Trail. They were about the same age and neither of them had the responsibilities of a wife and family. It is possible that Charles Parker was in that long line of mourners that followed the body of his friend. Perhaps he was among those that shed tears that day.

---

[1] -Santa Fe Weekly Gazette, April 10, 1858 - Courtesy The New Mexico Persons Collection, New Mexico State Records Center & Archives, Santa Fe, NM
[2] - Ibid.

Chapter 6
Troubled Times In The Territory

One can only guess at some of the activities of Charles G. Parker as a result of the clues left among documents still available. One such document is an interesting one in which he co-signed a bond with another man by the name of Alexander Hatch for ten muskets. The document reads like this—

"Know all men by these presents that we, Alexander Hatch and Charles G. Parker are held and bound unto A. Rencher, his heirs and assigns, in the final sum of two hundred dollars, for the payment of which we bind ourselves, our heirs and personal representatives by these presents, sealed with our seals, and dated this 22nd day of November, 1858.

"The condition of the above obligation is such that whereas the said A. Rencher has this day loaned to the said Hatch, ten muskets of the Public Arms of the Territory of New Mexico, for the defense and protection of his farm and property in the county of San Miguel against the Indians. Now if the said Hatch shall on demand, return the said muskets in good order and condition to said A. Rencher or in default thereof, shall pay the full value of the same, or of such as shall not be returned, then this obligation to be void, otherwise to remain in full force and effect."

The document was signed by Hatch and C. G. Parker.[1]

The circumstances that brought about this action was an effort to distribute sufficient weapons among the civilian populace to deter Indian raids on unarmed civilian settlements. The way the document is written up, however, causes the reader to lose sight of the fact that it is government weapons being distributed by an official of the state.

Unfortunately, we will never know if Charles G. Parker lost $200 out of this event. However, from other sources we can learn something of the other characters in this action. Abraham Rencher,

---

[1] - This document courtesy the New Mexico State Records Center and Archives, Santa Fe, NM

Governor of the Territory, was a lawyer. He was originally from North Carolina and had been a member of congress, and had also served as U. S. minister to Portugal. His administration suffered greatly because of the many Indian raids, which the military seemed unable to stop. One example of such was the July 30, 1860, raid which took place about 10 miles outside of Santa Fe. Several citizens were killed by a band of Navajos. Two days later a return attack was made by the citizens in which ten of the citizens were lost. They reported that twenty-five or thirty of the Indians were killed. The Indians continued with their raid as far north as Taos and escaped.[1]

As might be expected, Santa Fe was divided over the best way to handle the problems with the Indians. Governor Rencher had the support of one faction who favored independent action by the citizens under the direction of the governor. The bond that Charles Parker signed in behalf of his friend, Alexander Hatch, was a part of that action. This method was supported by territorial law and was a system that had been used previously. Colonel Thomas Fauntleroy, the departmental commander, objected to the use of civilian "Indian Fighters," and threatened to withdraw regular troops if the Governor authorized a volunteer campaign. It developed into a nasty scene when two companies of volunteers were raised and Fauntleroy refused to issue them either arms or ammunition.[2]

We know very little about Alexander Hatch that would help us understand why Charles G. Parker would willingly risk $200 on him. What we do know about him would, in fact, cause one to wonder if he was worthy of Parker's investment.[3] John Kingsbury relates some of the local gossip to his partner, James Josiah Webb. Some of the details of this account written on September 8, 1860, and

---

[1] -Ralph Emerson Twitchell, "Old Santa Fe," Chicago, 1925, pg. 368

[2] -Jane Lenz Elder & David J. Weber, "Trading In Santa Fe", Dallas, TX, 1996, Pg. 185, N. 36

[3] -Ibid., Pg. 233, 253 and 277. In these letters from John Kingsbury, writing from Santa Fe to his trading partner James Josiah Webb in "the States," Alexander Hatch is mentioned three times. The first reference (pg. 233) Kingsbury says of another merchant, "I have seen only one bill at wholesale go from his house that was about $1,000+ to old man (Alexander) Hatch." In the last reference (pg. 277) Kingsbury says, "Since my last (letter) I have got a settlement in full with old man Hatch." These references would imply that Hatch was involved to some degree in Santa Fe merchandising.

some of the persons mentioned have no connection with Charles G. Parker but a view of Alexander Hatch is included which helps us have a better understanding of him. Here's what was written—

"Ellison is about & just the same as ever. When they started for court at Las Vegas, the Judge (Benedict) & all hands were tight (i.e., drunk), the driver Bully Welch, Houghton & Col. Street. They had not reached the rock corral when Ellison got uneasy at the speed, thought they would never get to Pigeon's & took the lines from the driver. Did not drive 500 yards before he hit a stump & upset the whole crowd. The carriage was pretty badly broke but they made out to fix up & go on. In the turn over, Judge Benedict fell under the others & hurt his left arm pretty bad. It swelled up directly but they all thought it was not serious as he could move his fingers. Since he has got back & the swelling gone down, he finds that the small bone at the elbow was dislocated & is now set itself in the place it was (k)nocked too, and will be a permanent injury to him. He can use the arm but it will be stiff. The others got off with slight bru(i)ses. At the court old man Hatch was indited(sic) for putting his brand on cattle that were proved to be stolen, 9 head and all fresh branded."[1]

We are still without understanding as to why Charles G. Parker signed the bond for Alexander Hatch. Perhaps they were friends or even partners in some venture yet to be discovered. Maybe Charles G. Parker actually did this as a business venture, receiving a percentage as fee for participating in the bond.

To confuse us even more, documents exist to indicate that some two and one half years later, Parker again signed a bond in behalf of another individual for weapons from the Public Arms. If, from the sketchy information available, it can be concluded that Alexander Hatch was a man of questionable character, the second man was entirely different.

The document reads like this—

"Know all men by these presents that we, James Giddings as principal and C. G. Parker as security, are held and firmly bound unto Abraham Rencher, Governor of the Territory of New Mexico, and to

---

[1] -Jane Lenz Elder & David J. Weber, "Trading in Santa Fe," Dallas, 1996, Pg. 253. This volume gives one of the best views available of all that went into the enterprise of transporting tons of merchandise across the prairies and selling it, at both wholesale and retail, in Santa Fe.

his successors in office, in the sum of one hundred and fifty dollars, for the payment of which we bind ourselves, our heirs and personal representatives, by these presents, sealed with our seal and dated this 23rd day of April, A. D. 1861.

"The conditions of this obligation is such that, whereas, the said Abraham Rencher, Governor as aforesaid, has, in pursuance of the authority upon him conferred by law, this day issued and loaned to the said James Giddings, certain of the public arms of said Territory, to wit: eight muskets and two rifles. Now, if the said James Giddings shall well and truly return the said arms to the Governor of said Territory when return of the same shall be required of him, then this obligation to be null and void, otherwise to remain in full force and effect."

The document was signed by James Giddings and Charles G. Parker.[1]

James Giddings was a man whose name appears numerous time in the history of New Mexico. He was appointed as clerk of the court under Judge James Houghton the first American judge to hold court in Santa Fe. This was on December 1st, 1846.[2]

After the murder of Governor Charles Bent in January of 1847 when the revolt broke out in Taos, an emergency company of civilian fighters was formed to assist in quelling the revolution. This unit was formed with Ceran St. Vrain as captain. About five dozen other names are mentioned, both as officers and enlisted men. Two names catch our attention. Listed as a sergeant is Preston Beck, Jr., and among the privates is James Giddings.[3]

The mystery of Charles G. Parker's connection with James Giddings goes unresolved, but now we know that these three, Preston Beck, Jr., James Giddings, and Charles G. Parker would have all known each other. It was a small world then, also.

---

[1] - This document courtesy of the New Mexico State Records Center and Archive, Santa Fe, NM

[2] - Ralph Emerson Twitchell, "Old Santa Fe," Chicago, 1925, pg. 286

[3] - Ibid. pg. 282

Chapter 7
The Wagonmaster

No documents have been discovered that would give any clear understanding as to when Charles G. Parker left the employment of other freighters and began to operate his own train. We know that by the fall of 1859, Parker, now thirty-nine years old, was well known on the trail. S. N. Wood, editor of the Kansas Press, gave his readers this information in the November 7, 1859, issue[1] -

LATEST NEWS FROM THE PLAINS
Santa Fe Mail Just Arrived
Another Murder On The Plains

"The Santa Fe mail arrived in this place last evening from New Mexico. From T. K. McCutchen, of the firm of J. & W. R. Bernard of Westport, Mo., we are indebted for late news from the Plains.

"The first mail west since the Indian difficulties arrived at Ft. Union Oct. 19th, Peter Kelley, Conductor. This mail left Ft. Union, Oct. 21st, with an escort of 75 men, Captain Morris of the Rifles commanding. The escort came with them to the crossing of the Big Arkansas, the escort this side had left four days before, and the mail came through unprotected. The mail met Hickman's train at the Breaks of the Red River. Kitchen's train at the Point of Rocks. Majors & Russel's at White's Creek. Shoemaker's train at Round Mound. They met Col. Fontleroy's command and outgoing mail at Cottonwood Holes.

"Half of our escort returned with Col. Fontleroy. Capt. Jackson then escorted us to the Arkansas. Pat Cahill, the Conductor of the outgoing train, had just been killed by the Indians, on the Cimeron River, we did not learn the particulars. Met Whitlock's train at Cottonwood holes, **PARKER'S TRAIN** and outgoing Mail with Milligan Conductor, at middle Cimeron Springs. At Pawnee Fork found Capt. Stewart and eighty men, met Bent's train with two pieces of artillery at Big Bend of Arkansas. Met Peter Porter and Mail at Cow Creek. Besides Mr. McCutchen, Dr. DeLeon of U. S. Army,

---

[1] - "Kansas Press" - Council Grove, KS, November 7, 1859

and W. B. Tipton, of New Mexico, came (as) passengers. The Mail is in charge of James Woodruff, Conductor. The prospect now is that we shall have regular mails again, we breath easier."

We have recorded this item with the spelling and punctuation as it appeared in the newspaper. It was no doubt composed in the mind of the editor and set in type all at the same time. It reveals several very interesting facts for us. Obviously, it tells us a great deal about the movement across the plains. Train after train was met by the incoming mail. The item reveals that there was continued trouble with the Indians on the trail As our main point of interest, it mentions "Parker's train" which would let know that by this date Charles G. Parker had gone into freighting on his own, and in a big way as we shall see.

John Kingsbury made several off-handed references to Charles G. Parker in correspondence with his partner, James Josiah Webb. On October 24, 1858, he wrote, "I have rec.d B/L (bill of lading) of one case merchandise shipped by Parker #8587, 230 lbs. This is all the goods that I have notice of being shipped since you left West Port."[1] By November 20, 1858, he was able to report, "Parker just arrived and I have rec.d the case of goods from Jeffries & Sons but have not opened it. I just got it at dark."[2]

John Kingsbury expressed what might be considered anti-Semitic feelings toward some of his competition when he wrote this short statement a year later, on November 19, 1859[3] - "My sales so far this month have been very small. Parker's train got in a few days since. He brought freight for a new Jew house (store). They are straingers (sic), have got the house Henry Mercure occupied. They have a large lot of goods and a good assortment. This outfit dampens my prospects considerable."

The Council Grove newspaper took note of this young wagon master as he brought his train into town from the west, slowly plodding down main street to the ford on the Neosho, across the river and into camp in the grove on the east side. The item read, "C. G. Parker's train, consisting of 21 wagons, 225 mules, and 30 men, just

---

[1] - Jane Lenz Elder & David J. Weber, "Trading in Santa Fe", Dallas, TX, 1996, pg.119
[2] - Ibid. pg. 123
[3] - Ibid. - pg. 191

26

in from Las Vegas, New Mexico, passed through town on Wednesday last for Kansas City. Mr. Parker's wagons were loaded with Government stores. He also brought 18 passengers from New Mexico to the States."[1]

In less than ten years after he passed through Council Grove on that first trip west, Charles G. Parker had established himself in business as a freighter on the Santa Fe Trail. His name was known by many of his contemporaries, and no doubt he was a respected member of the fraternity of freighters. There were many adventures yet ahead of him before he would retire to his farm in the valley of the Neosho.

The Elsberg-Amberg wagon train in the Plaza in Santa Fe in October of 1861. (*Courtesy of the State Records Center and Archives, Santa Fe, McNitt Collection, photo #6846*)

---

[1] - This item from the "Kansas Press", Council Grove, KS, August 25, 1860, was recorded in "The History of Morris County - 1820 to 1890", by John Maloy, pg.30.

Chapter 8
The Slow-Turning Wheels of Justice

Nearly three years had passed since that spring day in 1857 when about 200 Kiowa Indians had attacked the wagon train of Beck & Johnson on the Kansas plains.[1] According to an act of Congress, passed in 1834, any citizen of the United States whose property was taken or destroyed by Indians had the right to petition for compensation from the federal government. If the particular Indian tribe in question was receiving annual payments from the government, the claim was to be deducted from that amount. Otherwise, it would be paid from the Treasury of the United States.[2]

James L. Johnson, the surviving partner of the firm of Beck & Johnson evidently felt that he had waited long enough for compensation so he did what any red-blooded American would do, he hired a lawyer. Not just any lawyer, you understand, but one of the premier legal minds in the territory, John S. Watts.

Judge Watts had been active in public affairs in New Mexico for many years. Originally from Indiana, he had been appointed to the territorial supreme court by President Millard Fillmore, thirteenth president of the United States. He was assigned to the 2nd district at Albuquerque, where he presided until 1854 when he was replaced by an appointee of the new president, Franklin Pierce. He then moved to Santa Fe where he opened a law practice.[3] He was still referred to as "Judge" as a courteous reference to his previous high office.

To be an attorney and a politician in early New Mexico could be both exciting and dangerous. Only the previous year, Judge Watts, while running for the office of Territorial Delegate, had found himself involved in a duel with his opponent, Miguel A. Otero. Watts had made a speech, charging the incumbent Otero with neglect of duty, a charge that was quite mild by today's conduct. Otero called Watts a

---

[1] - See chapter 4

[2] - This information pertaining to the laws involved and the actual claim and ultimate reconciliation thereof are from 37th Congress, 2nd Session, House of Representatives, Report C. C. No. 290, referred to as Serial Set #1146.

[3] - Ralph Emerson Twitchell, "Old Santa Fe," Chicago, 1925, pg. 349

liar, both in English and Spanish, in such a manner as was impossible for Watts to ignore it, according to the standards of the day. The challenge for the duel was issued, friends were enlisted to assist, and the event was set to take place at sunrise on the 7th of September, 1859. The weapons selected were Colt's navy six-shooters, one barrel loaded, at a distance of fifteen paces. After the first pull of the trigger, which fell on empty chambers in the weapons, friends of the two parties attempted to bring about a reconciliation. This effort failed, so two more shots were tried, with the same effect. The offended party declared himself satisfied, and the people all went home, probably because everyone recognized that the possibility of someone getting hurt had multiplied greatly.[1]

Judge Watts started his actions in behalf of James L. Johnson with a petition to the Court of Claims, reciting the events as they had taken place, ending with this statement, "Your petitioner, therefore, asks the court to report a bill providing for the payment of the value of the said property so destroyed, with interest thereon from the 1st of June, 1857. The said James L. Johnson, as said surviving partner, being the sole owner of said claim." This communication was dated, April 5, 1860.

This set into action a whole set of claims and counter-claims involving Judge Watts and the Secretary of the Interior in Washington, along with the Commissioner of the Office of Indian Affairs. The thrust of the communications boiled down to a claim by Judge Watts that the original claim for compensation had laid in someone's office without being acted on properly and promptly. The bureaucrats in Washington, meanwhile, insisted that the claimants had not jumped through all the necessary hoops, dotted all the "I's" and crossed all the "T's" properly.

Evidently John Watts had struck the proper notes in Washington because arrangements were made to take additional testimony on the case in Santa Fe. From our standpoint, the interesting thing about this meeting is that it gives us a first-person interview with Charles G. Parker. He is being questioned by Judge Watts, attorney for the claimant in the presence of R. H. Thompkins, attorney for the U.S. Government and David V. Whiting,

---

[1] - Oliver LaFarge, "Santa Fe," Norman, OK, 1959, pg. 9

commissioner. The meeting was at the office of Hon. A. M. Jackson, secretary of the Territory of New Mexico on November 15, 1860.

Let's listen in as Charles G. Parker is questioned and he answers in his own words—

Question 1. State your name, occupation, age, place of residence during the past year; whether you have any interest, direct or indirect, in the case in question; and whether, and in what degree, you are related to the claimant.

Answer. Charles G. Parker; freighter; thirty-six years of age; on the prairie; none; not related to the claimant in any degree.

Question 2. Were you in the employment of Messrs. Beck & Johnson at the time of the killing of two mules by the Indians; and if so, state when and where it was, and in what capacity you were then acting?

Answer. I was in the employment of Messrs. Beck & Johnson as wagon-master when two mules were killed by the Indians on the Arkansas, about the 25th of May, 1856 (should be 1857).

Question 3. Before the mules were killed, what articles had been delivered to the Indians, what was the value of said articles so delivered, and for what purposes and under what assurances were said articles delivered?

(Objected to, being leading)

Answer. We gave them some rice and crackers, some sugar, a box of tobacco, some fifty pounds of coffee, about ninety pounds of sugar, nearly a barrel of crackers, valued at fifty or sixty dollars, and were given the assurance that we would be allowed to proceed on our journey without molestation.

Question 4. What Indians were they to whom the above articles were given and by whom the mules were killed?

Answer The Kiowas.

Question 5. State the value of the mules killed and the circumstances under which they were killed, and to whom did the mules and other property belong.

Answer. They were not worth less than one hundred dollars each. The Indians followed the train for a distance of seven or eight miles, taking the blankets from the men and stealing articles from the wagons. Their bows were strung, and they would threaten to shoot the men if they did not give them their coats or knives or other articles of wearing apparel. They took some stretcher sticks (?) from the

30

wagons and dropped one, which I picked up and waited to throw it in the wagon; when I went to throw it in the wagon, some one endeavored to jerk it out of my hand. I turned to see who it was, and saw it was an Indian. I hit him over the head with the stick, knocking him down. By this time, the men had their guns prepared to fire upon the Indian, who jumped over a bank, getting out of sight. The chiefs then came up and told us that if we would give them some sugar, coffee, tobacco, and other articles, that they would tie the men who had annoyed us, and that we would be allowed to go on unmolested. We gave them the articles and traveled on. When rising a hill, two Indians came from the side of the road and shot two mules from the first wagon. The mules and other articles belonged to Beck & Johnson.

Question 6. Are you the same person who formerly gave your affidavit in regard to this matter to be sent to the Indian Department?
Answer I think I am.

This ended the questioning of Charles G. Parker on the matter of the Indian raid on the wagon train in May of 1857. An interesting sidelight to this matter is that the witness (Parker) received a fee of $1.50, but the Commissioner received a fee of $6.89.

Additional testimony was taken from other parties, including forty-seven year old Jacob Houghton, the attorney who had drawn up the partnership papers for the firm of Beck & Johnson. He testified that the firm did, indeed, own a wagon train and that Preston Beck, Jr., had died in April of 1858. Francisco Griego, the man who had been beaten by John Gorman, resulting in the death of Preston Beck, Jr.[1], gave his testimony through an interpreter. He received a fee of $2.50, the interpreter was paid $5.00, and the commissioner received $10.35.

John S. Watts filed a three-page brief restating the position of the claimants, seeking damages for the raid. In twelve pages, R. H. Gillet, United States Solicitor, responded in a way that would make his modern-day counterparts proud. He quoted numerous laws and treaties in an effort to show that the attack in which the mules were killed was really the fault of Charles G. Parker because he had hit one

---

[1] - See chapter 5.

31

of the Indians with that stretcher stick. His response was dated March 15, 1861.

Another nine months went by before J. Loring delivered the opinion of the Court of Claims which was dated December 9, 1861. In less than two pages it was declared that petitioners had followed the proper procedures in presenting the claim. One paragraph that is of interest to us reads as follows—

"So it was argued that the killing of the mules was provoked by one of the wagoners (Charles G. Parker) of the petitioner who struck one of the Indians, and that therefore the petitioner was not entitled to indemnity. But the evidence does not connect the two acts, and the blow was struck to repel the assault of the Indian who attempted to take the stretcher from the wagoner, and it was thus in self-defense, as far as the wagoner was concerned, and cannot forfeit the right of the petitioner who had nothing to do with it."

The report was concluded with this statement, "A bill will be reported to Congress that the petitioner is entitled to relief in the sum of two hundred and fifty dollars." How long it was before James L. Johnson finally received his money is not know. What we do know is that Charles G. Parker was declared innocent of provoking the killing of two mules in western Kansas in the spring of 1857.

Chapter 9
The Hotel Keeper

In pursuing the story of Charles G. Parker, some amazing facts have come to light, almost by accident. One such fact is that for a time in 1861 and 1862, Parker had forsaken the trail business to become proprietor of the Exchange Hotel in Santa Fe. We might wonder why he would have undertaken such an endeavor, but with a little background information, we can understand that though he was not on the trail itself, he was right in the middle of the activity in Santa Fe.

"The corner of San Francisco and Shelby Streets in Santa Fe is the oldest hotel corner in the United States."[1] That bold statement by Philip St. George Cooke III, writing under the pen name of Peter Hertzog, is apparently without historical basis. A number of other writers agree, however, that a hotel, or lodging house of some sort, had occupied the corner for many years. The simple truth is that there is no known record determining just when it was first established as a lodging place for travelers.[2]

Positioned as it was at the south east corner of the plaza, the Exchange Hotel, the United States Hotel, or La Fonda, as it was known at various times, was right at the end of the Santa Fe Trail. This would have put it in the middle of all of the bustle and activity of the city. Charles G. Parker would have only been a few steps from scenes never viewed in "the States." James Josiah Webb describes some of the goings-on like this[3] - "A Mexican *fandango* in those days was a curiosity. The *sala,* or dancing hall, was from twenty to thirty feet long, and fifteen to eighteen feet wide, with sometimes benches on the sides (but frequently without seats of any kind) and packed full, only leaving sufficient space through the center for the couples to waltz through, up and down. When the dance began, the men would

---

[1] - Peter Hertzog, "La Fonda, The Inn of Santa Fe' Santa Fe, 1964, Pg. 3

[2] - Marian Meyer, "Mary Donoho, New First Lady of the Santa Fe Trail" - Santa Fe, 1991, pg. 45

[3] - James Josiah Webb, "Adventures In The Santa Fe Trade - 1844-1847" - Lincoln, 1995, pg. 95

place themselves in line on one side, and when the line was complete, the women would begin to rise and take their positions opposite the men, almost always in regular order without manifesting any choice of partners; and when the numbers were equal, the music would strike up and the dance proceed.

"I have witnessed some most ludicrous scenes at these *fandangos*. It was not anything uncommon or surprising to see the most elaborately dressed and aristocratic woman at the ball dancing with a peon dressed only in his shirt and trousers open from the hip down, with very wide and full drawers underneath, and frequently barefoot, but usually with moccasins. And such disparity of ages! On one occasion I saw at a ball given by Governor Armijo an old man of eighty or over dancing with a child not over eight or ten. I could not help the reflection that it was literally a dance of the cradle and the grave. They do literally dance from the cradle to the grave. And I have never seen anything lascivious or any want of decorum and self-respect in any woman in a *fandango*, whatever might be her reputation for virtue outside. I have known of disorders and serious brawls in *fandangos*, but it was almost invariably where Americans and whiskey were found in profusion."

Ralph Emerson Twitchell, former Director of the Historical Society of New Mexico, has written the best description available of the Exchange Hotel and the activities surrounding it.[1] He says -

"The old structure was the most notable land-mark of the Santa Fe Trail during the "American" period. It was a one story building built around a *patio* with a large corral and stables on the south, where the trail connected with what was known as the Rio Chquito (the Water Street of today). It was the rendezvous of the trappers, traders, pioneers, merchants, soldiers and politicians down to the coming of the Santa Fe Railway. Its gaming tables were the lure for all classes of Santa Fe society and its liquid cheer soon gave to the "tenderfoot" sojourner all the courage, dash and dare-devil spirit of the true son of the mountains and plains."

This last statement is particularly interesting to us in our pursuit of knowledge of the activities of Charles G. Parker in Santa Fe, as we shall soon discover.

---

[1] - Ralph Emerson Twitchell, "Old Santa Fe," Chicago, 1925, pg. 237, note 481

Twitchell goes on,[1] "The main entrance was on the corner, which opened into the lobby or office. Immediately back of the office was a series of rooms fronting on what is now known as Shelby Street today, each of which had an outside as well as an inside entrance, one leading to the street and the other into the patio, on the south side of which was located the dining room, which communicated on the west with a large parlor or reception room. In all of these rooms one found the simplest kind of furniture in the earlier days, but after the Civil War the guest rooms and the parlor were well equipped. Immediately east of the office, or lobby, and connected with it with swinging screen doors was the bar, which opened also on San Francisco street, and on the south, through a wide opening, communication was had with the large *sala*, in which was to be found every kind of gambling game known in the West in those times, the principal games being *faro* and *monte*, and in the early days a game called *chusas*, the precursor of the roulette wheel of more recent times. Tables devoted to draw poker and other "short" card games were in evidence and two or three billiard tables. The room was about 24 feet wide by 50 feet or more in length and faced the patio. On San Francisco street, facing north, were several guest rooms and these also were used oftentimes for gaming purposes of a more private and select character, and for higher stakes than those in the main hall. In these private rooms magnificent midnight luncheons, the best which the town afforded, were served by the proprietors without cost to the players who were also accommodated with liquors and cigars on an equally liberal basis and without stint or exception. The public were excluded from these private quarters, dedicated to the goddess of chance.

"On three sides of the patio, there was a fine portal and all around were flowers and vines, and, as old timers will recall, several mocking-birds in cages swinging from the *vigas* of the *portales*. In the summer time it was not unusual, particularly when guests were numerous, to serve meals in the *patio* under the *portales*.

"There were two kitchens, one which connected with the dining room on the east, and another in the corral, the latter being used in the trail and stage-coach days by the teamsters and others who had corral privileges. The main entrance to the corral was on the

---

[1] Ralph Emerson Twitchell, "Old Santa Fe," Chicago, 1925, pg. 237, note 481

south near the corner of the Sisters of Loretto property. The stages from eastern points on arrival always made their first stop at the Fonda and thence to the post office, passengers being unloaded at the office entrance on the corner, which was the actual "end of the Santa Fe Trail."

The Exchange Hotel, c. 1858, in the middle of the picture, marked "1", with a residence, marked "3", at the left and the store of Seligman & Clever, marked "2", at the right.

(Courtesy Museum New Mexico, neg. no. 10685)

Our knowledge of Charles G. Parker's association with the Exchange Hotel comes about through a very interesting set of circumstances. Before we get to that, however, a bit of history to set the scene would be in order.

In the early stages of the Civil War, the Confederacy was attempting to extend it's influence as far west as possible. They hoped that, with the encouragement of U.S. Army officers with southern sympathies, the native New Mexicans might still be smarting sufficiently from the overthrow of Mexican authority less than twenty years earlier, to rise up and join the Confederacy.

36

"The Confederate leaders had evolved a great scheme so far as New Mexico and surrounding areas, including California, were concerned. They had planned the earliest possible possession of the immense mineral resources of the Rocky Mountain territory and California, thus supplying the Confederacy with resources which would serve as a basis of credit, both to currency and bonds, as well as furnish the raw material for the promotion of great manufacturing centers which would compare with those of the North in the New England states."[1]

Without detailing all of the military movements, it is sufficient to say that the "Army of New Mexico," under the command of the Confederate Brigadier General H. H. Sibley moved out of Texas and headed west. The uprising of the populace did not happen as they had hoped. Nevertheless, the westward movement of the southern forces continued, arriving in the area of Santa Fe in March of 1862.

General Sibley led his forces into Santa Fe, marching into and around the plaza. They took possession of the palace and of Fort Marcy, just outside the city. General Sibley, Col. A. M. Jackson and the rest of his staff were quartered at the Exchange Hotel. General Sibley missed two of the major military engagements in the area, the battles of Glorietta and Apache Canyon, however. He had been "overcome" by the generous supply of wine and brandy from the hotel bar.[2] Shortly thereafter, General Sibley, in council with his officers, decided to evacuate New Mexico and abandon their grand scheme of western conquest. They had been in Santa Fe about one month.[3]

We know that Charles G. Parker, now forty two years old, was the proprietor of the Exchange Hotel during that period of time. It is certain that he was in that position at least from the month of August in 1861 to August 12, 1862. Can we imagine that he sat there at the bar, offering the General "one more for the road," with the idea that he was having a hand in the defeat of the Southern forces? No records remain that would give us a clue to his thinking during that period of time. However, we can be sure that he was there, and that

---

[1] - Ralph Emerson Twitchell, "Old Santa Fe," Chicago, 1925, pg. 369
[2] - Ibid, pg. 238, note 481
[3] - Ibid, pg. 384

he was the proprietor of the Exchange Hotel because he and his friend, Francisco Griego, were in trouble with the law.

Charles G. Parker was charged with selling "spirituous liquors" to non-commissioned officers or enlisted men, according to a $200 bond that he was required to post on July 26, 1862.[1] The terms of the bond required that he should appear before the district court to answer those charges on the first day of their next term, which was to begin on the first Monday of August, 1862.

Two of the most influential Santa Fe merchants in town signed the bond with him. Siegmund Seligman and Levi Spiegelberg were a part of the small but prosperous Jewish merchant circle. Though anti-Semitism seemed to lurk in the hearts of some of their competitors,[2] they were well respected by the business community, as well as the military and civilian population.

The document pertaining to Charles G. Parker gives no details of the alleged crime. It does not list where the selling of liquor took place at, when the crime was committed, or any other facts about it. We would never know any more about the matter if it wasn't that his friend, Francisco Griego, found himself charged with perjury. This charge was apparently the result of his testimony at the trial of Charles G. Parker. An excerpt from the proceedings of the Grand Jury is as follows——

"The grand jurors for the Territory of New Mexico, taken from the body of good and lawful men of the County of Santa Fe aforesaid, duly elected, empowered, sworn and charged at the term aforesaid to inquire in and for the county of Santa Fe aforesaid, upon their oaths, do present that Francisco Griego, late of the county of Santa Fe in the Territory of New Mexico, on the 12th day of August in the year of our Lord One Thousand Eight Hundred and Sixty Two, at the county of Santa Fe aforesaid, the Grand Jury aforesaid, having

---

[1] - Territory of New Mexico v. Charles G. Parker, Santa Fe County District Court, Criminal Cases August 1862, State Records Center & Archives, Santa Fe, NM
[2] - Jane Lenz Elder & David Weber, "Trading In Santa Fe," Dallas, TX, 1996, pg. xxvii. John M. Kingsbury perceived them as a separate clique, referring to their enclave on one occasion as "our little Jerusalem of Santa Fe." Although the number of Jews in New Mexico in the 1850's was very small—perhaps sixteen in the 1850 census and thirty-six to forty-three in the 1860 census—nearly all were merchants or merchants' clerks.

then and there been lawfully organized, elected, empowered, sworn, and charged to inquire into and to investigate all violations of the laws of the Territory of New Mexico, committed within the county aforesaid and the said grand jury organized in manner and form and for the purposed aforesaid, on the twelfth day of August aforesaid under the direction of their foreman, Simon Delgardo, he the said Simon Delgardo then and there having for that purpose been legally sworn and qualified as such foreman, did then and there assemble and meet, for the purpose of performing and discharging the duties so required of them, and the investigations aforesaid, it then and there became a material question whether banking games prohibited by law had been permitted to be played and whether banking games such as monte, faro, pass faro, pass monte or other banking games prohibited by law had been played at a certain house, known as the Santa Fe Exchange, in the county aforesaid, of which **Charles G. Parker** was the proprietor and in which house spirituous liquors were sold, and for the purpose of making the investigation aforesaid, the said **Francisco Griego** was then and there duly called as a witness to testify before the said Grand Jury touching his personal knowledge in regards to violations of the law as aforesaid, and was then and there duly sworn and took his oath before the said Simon Delgardo, foreman of the Grand Jury."

The beautifully hand-written document continues with much additional flowery language until it comes to this statement - "**Francisco Griego** being so sworn as aforesaid, not having the fear of God before his eyes nor regarding the laws of this Territory, but being moved and seduced by the instigations of the Devil and contriving and intending to pervert the due course of the law and justice and to prevent the said Territory and her people from the prosecution of those who commit offenses against the laws of the said Territory. At and upon the examination and investigation aforesaid upon his oath aforesaid, falsely, corruptly, knowingly,..........did depose and swear among other things in substance and to the effect following, that is to say: that since the month of August in the year of our Lord One Thousand Eight Hundred Sixty One to the twelfth day of August, in the year of our Lord One Thousand Eight Hundred and Sixty Two, he, the said **Francisco Griego** had not seen or witnessed that any banking games prohibited by law as aforesaid, had been permitted to be played in the house called the Santa Fe Exchange, situated in the said county of Santa Fe, of which **Charles G. Parker**, was during the time aforesaid the proprietor and in which said house spirituous liquors were sold, and that he had not seen or witnessed that banking games prohibited by law.......had then and there been played, and that he, the said **Francisco Griego** did not know that in the house aforesaid during the time aforesaid games so prohibited by law had been played,....he had not entered any room or chamber in the said house in which games prohibited by law were then being played.........whereas in truth and in fact he the said **Francisco Griego** at the time he took his said oath well knew and during the time between the month of August 1861 and the twelfth day of August, 1862, banking games of the description aforementioned, prohibited by law had been permitted to be played and had been played in the afore described house of which **Charles G. Parker** was the proprietor and in which spirituous liquors were sold."

Unfortunately, we do not know how either of these two cases were reconciled. Neither do we know why Charles G. Parker was being held legally liable for activity that had apparently been a part of the Exchange Hotel's normal lifestyle for years. Three possibilities are present. Perhaps Charles G. Parker was seen as a Southern sympathizer because of something that took place during that month's occupation by the Confederate forces. Maybe Charles G. Parker was feeling the wrath of the civil government because of some licensing deficiency. Or it is possible that he was feeling a discretionary application of the law because of having fallen into disfavor with some local official.

Many things are uncertain about this whole affair, but one thing is positive - For a period of about a year, from the summer of 1861 to the summer of 1862, Charles G. Parker's life centered around the activities at the end of the trail as he served as the proprietor of the Exchange Hotel, also known as the Fonda.

Chapter 10
Back To The Trail

Those embarrassing events with the law in Santa Fe would be enough to make most men look for a friendlier climate, and that's just what Charles G. Parker did. We can only imagine how he sat about to conclude his business obligations in Santa Fe. He obviously didn't own the Exchange Hotel, but was only employed there. A complete listing of the various owners does not seem to exist, so we can't be sure of who his employer was. It is safe to assume there was no contract involved, so he probably just walked in one day and said, "I quit." Perhaps the words weren't quite that abrupt, but the effect was the same.

The next time we catch sight of Charles G. Parker, he's passing through Council Grove again. His outfit was a bit different this time though, and it probably caused quite a stir up and down main street.

Because it set astride the Santa Fe Trail, the town had seen it's share of unusual sights. About three years earlier, the local editor had reported[1] - 'WIND WAGON - The veritable wind wagon has at last arrived in this place from Westport, MO., a distance of 125 miles, propelled all the way by wind. It has sails somewhat similar to the sails of the schooners on our western lakes. Who says now that the Santa Fe road is not a navigable stream? We expect soon to see this wagon making regular trips between this place and Westport. Running time - 48 hours."

No other notice of this sailing vessel of the plains is recorded in later issues and we don't know who the captain was. Earlier records indicate that a similar vehicle, operated by a man named Thomas, had made the same journey in 1853.[2] He had attempted to form a company of investors with the idea of using the wind to travel the trail to deliver freight. He made the journey to Council Grove, and returned to Westport with a letter from a well-known Council Grove blacksmith as proof of his trip. His efforts to form the

---

[1] - "Council Grove (KS) Press", July 23, 1860
[2] -Stanley Vestal, "The Old Santa Fe Trail," Boston, 1939, pg. 4

company might have been successful, but a wrecked wind wagon ended it all. We know nothing more about Windwagon Thomas, but it may have been him who returned again in 1860 for one more try at the trail.

The year of 1863 was an extremely busy year on the Santa Fe Trail. G. M. Simcock, one of the merchants on main street of Council Grove, had kept a register of activity on the trail for the year. According to his figures, 3,000 wagons, 618 horses, 20,812 oxen, 8,046 mules, 98 carriages and 3,072 men were engaged in the freighting business along the trail that year. They transported over 15,000 tons of freight with an estimated value of over $40,000,000.[1]

During the early part of 1863, there was continuing fear of the guerrilla raids of the eastern border spilling into Morris County. Colonel S. N. Wood received proper authority from the Secretary of War and the Governor of Kansas to organize a home military force, called "Morris County Rangers." There fears were not without foundation as a raid was made on Diamond Springs in May of 1863.[2]

In addition to the activities centered on the Santa Fe Trail and the war, the Kaw Indian reservation was just a few miles outside of town. This created its share of excitement from time to time, as well as an occasional tense situation.

So the citizens of Council Grove were used to seeing some strange sights on Main Street, most of them going either east or west as a part of the commerce on that great highway of trade. The sight they saw early in October of 1863 may have been just a bit different than the usual. The local editor reported the event like this - "C. Parker & Co. passed through the Grove Thursday last, with 500 head of cattle for New Mexico."[3]

While this little item gives us one more glimpse of the trail activity of Charles G. Parker, it creates more questions than it answers. We might wonder if these 500 head of cattle were destined to become beef steak and hamburger for the army stationed in New Mexico. If that was the case, was Parker driving them for someone else, or was he the contractor, himself?

---

[1] - John Maloy, "History of Morris County - 1820 - 1890," - pg. 47
[2] - Ibid. - pg. 45
[3] - "Council Grove Press." Monday, October 5, 1863

A second possibility was that these cattle were oxen being driven to New Mexico as replacements for trains that had suffered stock loss on the way out. If this was the scenario, we would again wonder if Charles G. Parker was the investor, or if he was working for someone else.

A third, and perhaps the most unlikely possibility is that they were dairy cows headed to a ready market in New Mexico. In 1858 Hezekiah Brake made a trip over the trail to a ranch near Fort Union that was owned by Mr. Don Aleandro. He was employed as dairyman on the ranch.[1] He mentions that they were milking forty cows,[2] but also tells of the owner buying ten additional milk cows.[3]

Nothing certain can be known about the cattle that were being taken across the plains in the fall of 1863, but the very idea of taking that many cattle that far would leave us to wonder if it wasn't the most frustrating trip that Charles G. Parker ever made to Santa Fe.

---

[1] - Hezekiah Brake, "My Life On Two Continents," Topeka, 1896 - pg. 135
[2] - Ibid. pg. 143
[3] - Ibid. pg. 140

Chapter 11
On To Chihuahua

In considering the Santa Fe Trail, we usually picture in our minds long wagon trains moving across the plains to Santa Fe, unloading the merchandise there, and returning to "civilization" empty and ready to load up again. While this impression may be true, to a point, the activity of the trail was much broader.

In the introduction to their book, "Trading In Santa Fe," Jane Lenz Elder and David J. Weber point out that the trail was in fact an international commercial route, supplying Mexicans, both in New Mexico and beyond, with inexpensive yet well-made goods. The ordinary things of life, such as hardware and cloth, were hard to come by and the incoming wagons carried great treasures of such things to a ready market. These goods were paid for with silver from the mines of northern Mexico. Very soon the lure of great profits attracted merchants from both countries. Wagons headed west with great loads of merchandise destined for Santa Fe and the surrounding villages and on south to Chihuahua and other markets in that area. Meanwhile, Mexican merchants began moving up the trail with their own goods headed for Missouri. Some of these international travelers continued on to such points and Philadelphia and New York, buying American goods to haul back to their homeland, themselves.[1]

This opportunity for trade on farther south was enhanced by international intrigue, also. The editor of the Santa Fe Gazette noted in the summer of 1864, "Our merchants have sold, during the season, large stocks of goods to the merchants of Chihuahua. Since the blockade of the Mexican ports by the French, New Mexico offers the most convenient and best market to the traders of Chihuahua. Ten cents per pound is paid in gold from Santa Fe to the city of Chihuahua."[2]

This short statement includes a reference to a historical event not known by most twentieth-century Americans. That event was the

---

[1] - Jane Lenz Elder & David J. Weber, "Trading In Santa Fe," Dallas, TX, 1996, pg. xix
[2] - Santa Fe Gazette, July 20, 1864

effort made by France to set up an empire in the Western Hemisphere. It came about as a result of the ambitions of Napoleon III, Emperor of France, to emulate the military success of his famous uncle, Napoleon Bonaparte.

Without reciting all details involved, in 1864 France declared Mexico a French empire with Maximilian I, of Austria, as emperor. This was in defiance of the Monroe Doctrine which France would probably not have attempted had not the United States been occupied with the Civil War. At the close of the war General Philip Sheridan marched to the Rio Grande, and the French troops withdrew from Mexico. Maximilian was captured by the Mexicans and was shot in June of 1867.

Because of the ambitions of that French emperor, there was a ready market some five hundred miles south of Santa Fe that enticed many traders, including Charles G. Parker, to make that long and dangerous journey. No information is available as to the number of trips he may have made to Chihuahua, but one in particular proved to be most dangerous. "The New Mexican," printed in Santa Fe carried this item on August 12, 1864 -

"INDIAN OUTRAGES are becoming of frequent occurrence. An express arrived in town Tuesday last, bringing information that the train of Charles G. Parker, which left here about two weeks ago for Chihuahua, had been attacked by Indians, and the mules taken. We are indebted to Mr. Stevens, who had the letter from the wagon master in his possession, for the following particulars: The train was camped about twenty miles below the Gallinas Mountains, and while driving the mules to water, the Indians (supposed to be Mescalero Apaches,) made their attack and run off all the animals but five. The wagon master, Lovell, with some of his men, mounted the remaining animals and pursued the Indians for about a mile, when the latter dismounted, drove their horses and mules into the timber, and formed for a fight. The encounter was of the most desperate nature, the combatants being at times within a few yards of each other, and lasted until Lovell received two severe wounds in the hip, and one of his men had his leg broke by a ball above the ancle (sic), when they returned to the train. The letter states that they are twenty miles from permanent water, and that unless it rains or assistance arrives, they will be compelled to abandon the train."[1]

A number of questions come to mind in reading the account of this unfortunate event, but foremost would be - Was Charles G. Parker with his wagon train at the time of the attack? The fact that he wasn't mentioned in the news account would lead us to believe that he was not at the scene at the time of the attack. However, the actions that follow shortly would convince us that he was somewhere in the vicinity. Charles G. Parker, now forty-four years old, did what any red-blooded American pioneer would have done.....He went after his mules.

---

[1] - This item from the August 12, 1864, issue of "The New Mexican" is mentioned on pg. 25 of "Santa Fe, The Autobiography of a Southwestern Town" by Oliver La Farge, Norman, OK, 1959

Chapter 12
The Case Of The Missing Mules

The summer of 1864 saw a great amount of Indian trouble in the Territory of New Mexico. A letter from Fort Sumner,[1] southeast of Santa Fe, dated August 4, 1864, and addressed to the editor of the Santa Fe Gazette, told this unhappy story -

"Day before yesterday an expressman arrived here from Lieut. Newhold (with the news) that a band of hostile Apaches had made an attack near Chaparita, and that after killing and wounding several persons, they captured several women and children, and struck out in the direction of the Sierra Blanca Mountain. Capt. Fritz was detailed, on receipt of this intelligence, with 18 men of his company, and he started in the same direction in the hope of intercepting them.

"The same night an express arrived from Delgadito Chiquito, a Navajo Chief, stating that he had just seen the hostile Indians retreating with their plunder. This was near the Alamo Gordo. Capt. Gorham, Cal. Cav. Vols., and thirty-three of his Company were detailed at once to pursue them, and he left this Post about midnight.

---

[1] - My thanks to Mr. Harold C. Meyers, Superintendent of the Fort Union National Monument, Watrous, NM, for the following material about Fort Sumner which is from "Soldier and Brave, Historic Places Associated With Indian Affairs And The Indian Wars In The Trans-Mississippi West," published by the National Park Service in 1971 , pg. 229 - "Fort Sumner was founded in 1862 at Bosque Redondo ("Round Grove of Trees") along the Pecos River in Eastern New Mexico to guard the 400 Mescaleros and 8,000 Navajos conquered by Col. Kit Carson in 1862-64. In 1865, the Mescaleros, who detested the Navajos, fled. Three years later the U. S. Government commissioners who had earlier concluded the treaties at Fort Laramie, WY, and Medicine Lodge, KS, negotiated a treaty with the Navajos at Fort Sumner that allowed them to return to their ancestral homeland in northern Arizona. From 1866 through the early 1870's, Fort Sumner was a way station on the Goodnight-Loving Cattle Trail. Herds wintered near the fort, and were sometimes purchased by the government for issue to the reservation Indians. In 1869, the year after the Navajos departed, Fort Sumner was demilitarized and put up for auction. The New Mexico cattle king Lucian Maxwell purchased it and remodeled some of the buildings for residential and ranching purposes. On his death, his son Peter inherited the property. In 1881 Pat Garrett shot and killed "Billy the Kid" in the ranch house. His grave is in a small cemetery about a mile east of the deserted fort site."

At the same time, Capt. Calloway (also) left, (being) in charge of a number of Navajos who volunteered to go with him.

"Yesterday morning at 9 o'clock a.m. another express arrived with the following news: Delgadito, the Navajo Chief, who first sent word that he had seen the Indians, consulted with his men and the result was that they determined to attack the Apaches at once, and before the troops came up. Delgadito stated that his reason for this step was to show the Great Father that the Navajos were true friends. He formed his men and after a half an hour's ride overtook the Apaches, made a sudden charge and recaptured all the sheep, 4,000 in number, and the captives. The Apaches fled in confusion and Delgadito started to return home to the reservation. The Apaches, however, rallied soon after and having pursued the Navajos, overtook them and made a sudden attack. Delgadito fought bravely, but fortune abandoned him this time and he was obliged to fly, leaving four of his warriors dead on the field. He was wounded himself with three arrows and a rifle ball, and it is feared the noble fellow will expire today. Four of his braves were also wounded. Delgadito was brought in here yesterday, and last night he called his people together to hear his last words—as he did not expect to live till morning."

In the same issue the editor made this comment - "Indian Depredations: - The loss of the sheep which is mentioned by our Fort Sumner correspondent, and the loss of his mules by Mr. Parker near Fort Defiance[1] will suffice to remind the people of the eastern border of the Territory that there is a party of the Mescalero Apaches that has never been captured and that all the time during the past eighteen months has been prowling on that border. They, as we have several times mentioned in these columns, number about seventy or eighty, and have never been brought to terms of peace."

---

[1] - "Soldier And Brave," National Park Service, 1971, pg. 68 - "The name of this fort typifies the attitude of its garrison and that of the Navajos it sought to control. Only three miles west of the Arizona-New Mexico boundary, it was the first Army post in Arizona. After the failure of several treaties with the restive Navajos, who had terrorized residents of the southwest since Spanish times, Fort Defiance was founded to quiet them. In 1858, until which time only intermittent skirmishing had occurred, hostilities became intense. Two years later, 1,000 Navajos besieged the fort but were unable to capture it."

Not only were there Indian troubles in New Mexico, but there were continued attacks on the trains crossing the plains. The Santa Fe Gazette editor listed some of the military moves being made in that direction. He said, "In consequence to the continued and formidable hostilities of the Indians of the plains, Gen. Carleton had determined to use all the available military force in his Department to assist in restraining them from the commission of depredations. He has consequently ordered fifty cavalry and fifty infantry with two howitzers to the crossing of the Arkansas, fifty cavalry and fifty infantry to the lower Cimarron Spring, fifty cavalry and thirty infantry to the upper Cimarron Spring, a company of infantry to Fort Lyon to assist the troops stationed there and another company to Gray's Ranch to help escort the mail from Maxwell's to Fort Lyon."[1]

This was an extremely difficult time in the history of New Mexico. In spite of continued and increasing prosperity of the region, there was, for a period of about twenty years, almost constant warfare with the Mescalero Apaches and the Navajos. During the Civil War period, volunteer regiments were called upon for most of the efforts to control the Indians. A large number of New Mexicans achieved considerable notice because of their exploits in battle. Col. Kit Carson is perhaps best known among these, receiving most of the credit of the ultimate subjugation of the outlaw bands.[2]

A long and very detailed official communication was published in the September 3, 1864, issue of the Santa Fe Gazette. It was signed by Capt. F. McCabe, Commanding Officer of the 1st New Mexico Cavalry. He details his efforts to follow orders from Col. Kit Carson "to pursue and chastise a war party of Apaches who had lately committed various murders and robberies." He says, "I started accordingly and on the 11th reached Fort Stanton, where I was advised that the same body of Indians had attacked Mr. Parker's train near Gallinas Springs and ran off all his mules."

Captain McCabe's report continued with his efforts to hire guides, a record of their movements, including a march of 60 miles in twenty-four hours, and the trouble they encountered in finding drinking water. "Half of my command's horses were still in the

[1] - Santa Fe Gazette, September 3, 1864
[2] - Ralph Emerson Twitchell, "Old Santa Fe," Chicago, 1925, pgs. 385, 386

desert when I reached the (water) tanks and I immediately sent back water to their relief and at noon marched to a stream called Rio Alamo. I found here that most of my horses were broken down, they were abandoned by my order, and several of my men sick. We rested that day and sent the guide to Dog Canyon to look for the Indians."

The guide returned the next morning with the information that the Apaches were in the canyon. The Captain then detailed Lieutenant Gilbert and twenty men to follow their trail, "using diligence and caution in the pursuit." Meanwhile he said, "I marched my broken-down men and horses to a camp near Tularosa to recruit."

While he was at Tularosa, "Mr. Parker reached me yesterday informing me that Major Chacon had arrived, and I started again with sixteen of my men and fourteen citizens (the result of his recruiting efforts) to follow the Indians. On my way to this place, I met a messenger informing me that Lieut. Gilbert had a fight with the Apaches yesterday near Rio Milagro and that the Lieutenant was killed at the first discharge. All the horses were killed and wounded by the Apaches, and the guide and one man mortally and three privates of my company severely wounded." He then finished his communication with these words, "Although repulsed, the men of Lieut. Gilbert's party behaved nobly and he fell gallantly himself at the head of his men. I deeply regret his fall, and will avenge it if at all possible."

We know that the women and children taken captive were recovered by the Navajo Chief, Delgadito, in his ill-fated attack. We also know that the sheep were recovered[1], which had belonged to a Mr. Gonzales. Unfortunately, we also know that Charles G. Parker's mules were still missing because a short news item in the September 10, 1864 issue of the "Santa Fe Gazette" continues the story for us - "We understand that Mr. C. G. Parker has returned from the pursuit of the Indians who stole his mules, and that he reports to have seen them but in consequence of the manner in which they were mounted and arrned, it was impossible to retake the animals. The Indians who committed the robbery, it is said, were Coyotero Apaches and made their way to the San Francisco Mountains."

---

[1] "Santa Fe Gazette", Sep. 10, 1864

Additional information about the pursuit of the Apaches and the efforts to recover the mules is found in the journal of Major Rafael Chacon.[1] He writes in great detail, almost with the attitude of defending himself from some unknown charge. His entry for August 16, 1864, says - "I received instructions from Dept. Headquarters, ordering me to start out in person in pursuit of the said Indians, and also Lieut. Cook in command of his men. As I knew how things were at the Post, I stated to Mr. Parker that it would be advisable to wait the arrival of troops for the Garrison, and that I would in the meantime prepare for a prosecution of the Indians, which would insure the recovery of the mules, and that it was possible that Captain McCabe and Lieut. Gilbert might recover them. Mr. Parker replied that he would go in pursuit himself in case he should not have any other assistance, and also uttered some other improper words, perhaps somewhat excited at the loss of his mules. In view of this, I prepared my departure for 3 o'clock p.m."

Obviously, Charles G. Parker had lost patience with the efforts of the military to recover his mules. In addition to the time he had wasted chasing Indians and mules, it was a considerable financial loss to him. In the "Synopsis of Indian Scouts And Their Results For The Year Of 1864,"[2] it is revealed for the first time that about fifty mules were lost in that raid on the Parker wagon train on the way to Chihuahua. Nothing appearing in that scout report, or in any other place, indicates that any of the mules were ever recovered.

---

[1] - "Santa Fe Gazette", October 1, 1864
[2] - "Santa Fe Gazette", March 18, 1865

Chapter 13
Changing Times

By the fall of 1864, changes were beginning to be felt all across America. The conflict that had divided the nation was in the process of being brought to a close. In March of that year, General Grant had become Commander in Chief of all Federal forces and moved his headquarters to Virginia. He realized that the long fighting had severely weakened the forces of the South so he began a relentless campaign across all fronts. During those months that Charles G. Parker was searching all across New Mexico for his mules, the Civil War was increasing in intensity. Throughout the South, battle after battle turned into a rout. Finally, with his army depleted and his supplies exhausted, General Lee surrendered to Grant at Appomattox Court House, Virginia, on April 9, 1865.

Other changes were about to take place, also. The Civil War had, for the most part, suspended westward movement of the railroads but that was about to change. Cyrus K. Holliday, future Senator Edmund G. Ross, and two other Topeka residents had gone by buggy on September 14, 1860, to Atchison, KS, where they officially formed what was to become the Atchison, Topeka & Santa Fe Railroad.[1] Although it was still a number of years away from putting the Santa Fe Trail out of business and into the pages of history, it was on the way.

Old ways die hard sometimes, and in the case of a town's commerce, it was up to the local editor to keep the community spirits high. Consequently, it's not surprising that the Council Grove (KS) Democrat carried these items in July and August of 1866—

July 6, 1866 - "TRAINS MOVING - For the past two weeks, trains have been moving constantly. From twenty-five to fifty per day, heavily loaded, have passed out, en route for New Mexico."

Aug. 4, 1866 - "On Saturday last, Ladrick & Robbins (local merchants in Council Grove) loaded seven wagons with goods for the west, on Monday, two wagons, and on Tuesday and Wednesday, five

---

[1] - Keith L. Bryant, Jr. - "History Of The Atchison, Topeka and Santa Fe Railroad," Lincoln, 1982, pg. 8

wagons for New Mexico. Our other merchants are also doing a lively business."

Aug. 18, 1866 - "TRAINS MOVING - A large number of trains have passed through, westward bound, during the past week, and quite a number going in (to the east)."

Back in New Mexico, we might wonder what Charles G. Parker was thinking about as he chased his mules all over the Territory. If our earlier guess that he had visited the upper reaches of the Neosho River during one of his stops in Council Grove was correct, he might have fondly remembered that peaceful valley. Is it possible that he might have said to himself, in the vernacular of the late twentieth century, "I'm outta here!!"? We'll never know for sure about that.

We do know that a rather cryptic announcement began to appear in the Santa Fe Gazette. It was carried the first time in the issue of October 15, 1864 and continued for several weeks. The announcement read like this –

DISSOLUTION OF PARTNERSHIP

The partnership heretofore existing between John Dold and Charles G. Parker, under the firm name of Dold & Parker, has been dissolved by mutual consent of the parties. Neither of the partners of said firm are authorized to use the name of the firm hereafter except in the settlement of the business of the firm.

Signed - John Dold and Charles G. Parker.

This single item is all that we know about this partnership between John Dold and Charles G. Parker. We do know that John Dold was a merchant in Santa Fe. John Kingsbury, in writing to his partner, James Josiah Webb, on October 1, 1859, said, "I have just sold a bill on 6 mos. To John Dole (Dold), perhaps it will come to something over $1,500.+ - prices low, but I could not let a safe man go past."[1] Several other references were made to him in their correspondence over the months ahead. Was it possible that Charles G. Parker and John Dold were partners in that wagon train that lost

---

[1] - Jane Lenz Elder & David J. Weber, "Trading in Santa Fe." Dallas, TX, 1996, pg. 181

fifty mules to the Indians? Were they in partnership in a retail or wholesale business wherein Charles G. Parker was freighting in the merchandise to Santa Fe and John Dold was selling it? Perhaps they were in a partnership of some other nature, such as a drinking and gambling establishment. We may never know the exact nature of their partnership, but it would seem that Charles G. Parker was bringing his ties to Santa Fe to a conclusion.

Although the Santa Fe Trail would yet see many months of activity before the railroad finally arrived, the handwriting was on the wall. Charles G. Parker was not alone in his recognition of the changes in New Mexico. The mark of a good businessman was the ability to know when to get in, and when to get out. Probably no one in Santa Fe was surprised when this little advertisement appeared in the Santa Fe Weekly Gazette of November 10, 1866—

TRAIN FOR SALE

A train of eleven wagons, of four to six American mules each, all complete and in good condition for service, for sale.

Inquire for particulars at Spiegelberg Bros.

Chapter 14
The Valley of Peace

The Neosho River has it's beginnings in the western part of Morris County, Kansas. As it moves southeast, picking up the waters of a number of creeks and springs, it quickly enlarges to a fair-sized stream. Differing from other rivers in Kansas that have their beginnings in the western part of the state, the Neosho is not a sandy river. However, the soil in the valley is a loose, black loam that will produce abundant crops of every kind.

In was in this valley, at a spot between where Clary Creek (called Parker Creek on some maps) flows into the Neosho from the north and Haun Creek comes in from the south, that Charles G. Parker settled down to live out the rest of his life.

As with so many of the details of his life, it is difficult to pin-point an exact date and say that this is when Charles G. Parker left the Trail and took up the life of a farmer/stockman/town-builder. In fact, some local family histories suggest that there were those in the community that made trips with him on the Santa Fe Trail. This probably would have taken place after he had made the initial move into the valley.

The recorded history of the area actually begins many years earlier, when a young man by the name of Peter Baum signed up to become a Private in Captain Wolf's Company, Ohio Militia, to serve in the War of 1812. An act of Congress that was passed on March 3, 1855, granted bounty land to officers and soldiers who had engaged in the Military Service of the US. Consequently, warrant number 31,805 for 160 acres of land was deposited in the General Land Office in favor of Peter Baum. At that point, he owned the land that later contained the farmstead and townsite of Charles G. Parker's town, Parkerville. Whether Peter Baum ever visited the area is uncertain, but for some reason he assigned his warrant to another man by the name of Granville Coulter. Thus, on September 1, 1860, President James Buchanan signed a patent in favor of Granville

Coulter. Now he owned the land which later contained the farmstead and the townsite of Parkerville.[1]

Prior to this date, a family by the name of Black had moved into the area, also. Thomas Black and his wife, Priscilla Craft Black, had come from White Sulfur Springs, West Virginia, to take a claim east of the Parkerville townsite area in 1855.[2] One of their sons, William, became owner of the townsite area. He built the first house in what later became Parkerville. It was a log cabin that sat on the hill just inside the west city limits on the south side of the road. A local news item mentioned this little log house many years later like this - "Mrs. Rinard has purchased the L. McKenzie property in the north west part of town. This is the oldest house in the valley, and was built by Uncle Billy Black in the early '60's."[3]

When Charles G. Parker came to the valley, apparently in 1866, he soon purchased the William Black property, along with the log cabin, and made it his home until the large stone house that was so closely identified with him for many years was being constructed. Over a period of time he purchased various parcels of farm land until he had put together holdings of 400 acres, 200 acres under cultivation, 100 acres of timber, and the balance in pasture.[4]

Charles G. Parker, still only forty-six years old, was now ready to settle down in that peaceful spot in the valley that, beyond doubt, he had viewed years earlier during a stop in Council Grove. Before we move our narrative into the Parkerville years, there is one additional detail to be brought to our attention. It ties his life on the trail together with his life in the valley, but more than that, it shows that he had, even in those early years as well as in the later ones, a charitable heart for those in need.

---

[1] - Land Abstract - Author's collection.
[2] - Ramsey Black Record, 1796-1961 by Edna Clymer Sample
[3] - "Parkerville (KS) Times," Feb. 6, 1896
[4] - A. T. Andreas, "History Of The State Of Kansas," Chicago, 1883, pg. 808

Chapter 15
The Orphan

Most people living in the area around Parkerville have heard a legend about Charles G. Parker that always lacked substantiation. The legend took on various forms and shapes, but usually had these elements - When Charles G. Parker settled in Parkerville he had an Indian wife and a half-breed son who later ran off. Because of the date of his first marriage in 1867, to be discussed in the next chapter, this seemed highly unlikely, but still the story wouldn't die.

Happily, a news item has surfaced[1] that carries the true story of Charles G. Parker's "adopted" Indian son. It is from the June 19, 1891, issue of the "Council Grove Republican," printed in Council Grove, KS. The "Republican imp" is obviously a reference to the reporter for the newspaper who followed the procession. The item, in it's entirety, reads as follows—

DEATH
IN THE HAPPY HUNTING GROUND
C. G. PARKER'S ADOPTED INDIAN BOY

"On last Tuesday morning about 10 o'clock an ambulance was seen going west on main street; in the seat were two men and in their rear was a coffin. There were no mourners following in solemn procession, and as the wagon moved along slowly up the street a Republican imp, whose curiosity had been aroused by the appearance of the mysterious wagon, was seen following in it's wake, when opposite Greenwood Cemetery the sexton swung wide open the great iron gate and the wagon turned and passed through the arched entrance into the city of the dead.

"Along the beautiful drives, ornamented on either side with evergreens and sweet scented flowers, the lonely wagon moved until the potter's field was reached, then halted in front of a freshly dug grave. The coffin was lifted from the vehicle and lowered into the grave; as the clods rattled upon the coffin lid, no prayer was heard to

---

[1] - My thanks to Sue Metcalfe of White City, who not only told me of the existence of this news item but loaned me her copy

ascend for the welfare of the spirit which had so recently taken its departure from that body of clay. Not a tear was shed, for those present were not employed as mourners, their mission was simply business. When the grave had been filled, the leader of the funeral informed the news man that the lately interred coffin contained the remains of "INDIAN JUAN," a character who was well known in Morris County and whose death will be a surprise to many. He died at the county farm after suffering untold agonies for over a month with a disease of the stomach.

"The deceased was a half-breed Apache Indian and Mexican, and about 30 years of age. He was brought to Morris County when a papoose by Uncle Charley Parker, who picked the little waif up on a battle field in New Mexico, where he had been left by his routed people to the mercy of the coyotes. Although the little Indian was as hard to handle as a grizzly bear cub, Uncle Charley wrestled with him until he reached manhood and succeeded in doing a pretty good job of civilizing (him). Juan was well liked by all who knew him, and notwithstanding the bad composition he was composed of, he never was known to do a mean trick; he was a good worker, a natural mechanic and was very witty. He would not stick at one thing very long, but wherever he worked, he always had the confidence of his employers. As he never saved anything for a rainy day or gazed into the future—a mistake that many of the young pale faces are also making—he died in the poor house and sleeps in a pauper's grave. He is buried in Greenwood cemetery."

Even with the information found in this news item, questions exist. For example, did Charles G. Parker raise this boy in his home in Parkerville? This seems unlikely as no news items have been observed about him in the Parkerville newspapers. Perhaps he was placed with other Indians living in the area around Council Grove. Other information about him may exist, unknown to this writer, but what we do have gives us a bit of insight into the character of Charles G. Parker. His charitable spirit would be more obvious in later years.

Chapter 16
Time To Take A Wife

Sometime soon after Charles G. Parker settled in the valley of the Neosho, he began to court a young lady named Charlottie. Her maiden name was Parker, also, but was part of a family that had emigrated in from Virginia somewhere around 1860. Her brothers, Frank, Bill and Drury, all settled in the valley. Some of Bill's descendents still live in the area. An interesting item is that the marriage license[1] indicates that Charlottie's last name was "Scudder." Apparently she had been married previous to coming to the valley.

On March 26, 1867, 47-year old Charles G. Parker took as a bride, the 23-year old Charlottie. The were married at Clark's Creek, probably at the settlement there called "Far West," by Justice Of The Peace William M. Walter, who was the first postmaster there. He was most likely the closest man in the area who was authorized to perform a marriage ceremony.

We can only guess that they began their married life in that small log cabin on the hill on the west side of town, but very soon a brand new house was in construction. It was a large stone structure that gave plenty of room to entertain guests.

Mrs. Priscilla Moore, along with her brothers and sisters who were the children of Mr. and Mrs. W. H. Haun, was raised in that house in later years. She gave this description of the house. - "That fascinating structure contained eight rooms, two stairways, two chimneys, and four fireplaces. In that day, the number of chimneys that a house had stood for prestige. The more a person had on his house, the higher in rank he was regarded. The chimneys of the Parker house were built only in the north section of the house, one on the east and one on the west side of the house. There were four fireplaces in the north section, too, with two upstairs and two downstairs. There were two stairways in the house. The one in the north section of the house was a beautiful walnut open and winding stairway dividing the north section into two parts, both upstairs and

---

[1] - This document is from the archives of the office of the Clerk of the District Court, Court House, Council Grove, KS

downstairs. The stairway in the south section was more ordinary and quite steep. The unique idea in having the two stairways was the division of the house. It was possible to go from the north section to the south section when downstairs, but there was no opening between the north and the south when upstairs, so it was necessary to come back down again to go up again. It is possible that the house was so divided and designed as it was used as an inn at the time by the builder, Mr. Parker."[1]

Charles G. Parker's big stone house where so many people found real frontier hospitality. (*Author's Collection*)

The history of the house as an inn is uncertain, but one thing is sure.......there were a multitude of guests, both temporary and those of a more permanent nature. The 1900 Federal Census, enumerated by Richard Varner, listed seven people as residents of the Charles G. Parker household as of June 7th of that year. They included Charles G. Parker and wife; Clara Johnson, age 17, listed as

---

[1] - Interview with Mrs. Priscilla Moore by Jeri Blythe Bothwell - 1965

a servant; Lewis McKenzie, age 54, a boarder; Bert Stone, age 16, a servant; Frederick Stone, age 25, a boarder; and Harry Stone, age 27, also a boarder.

At this point in his life, Charles G. Parker settled down from the uncertain life of the trail and became a well-respected citizen of the county. He was elected to serve as State Representative from Morris County but there is some doubt about the exact year that he won the election. It may have been 1869[1], 1870[2], or 1872[3], but it seems certain that he served at least one term.

During this time, he also became involved in the county banking scene. In July of 1870, he, along with G. M. Simcock, W. A. McCollom, T. S. Huffaker, W. F. Shamleffer, W. R. Terwilliger, A. J. Hughs and J. W. Simcock, organized the Council Grove Savings Bank. They elected G. M. Simcock as president, T. S. Huffaker as vice-president, and J. W. Simcock as cashier. It was organized with a capital of $75,000.[4] Apparently, this business venture did not go as smoothly as might be hoped. In the October, 1872, district court news this item appeared - "Council Grove Savings Bank vs. Chas. G. Parker. Judgment for plaintiff, $699.73."[5]

We can only speculate about the plans that Charles G. Parker had formulated in his mind in previous years, but evidently at some point, perhaps while he was chasing the Indians who had stolen his mules in New Mexico, he said to himself, "I want to go back to that little valley on the Neosho River and start a town. I'll call it Parkerville."

---

[1] - John Maloy, "History of Morris County - 1820 to 1890." pg. 64

[2] - Obituary - Council Grove Guard - September 17, 1909

[3] - A. T. Andreas - "History of The State Of Kansas," Chicago, 1883, pg. 808

[4] - John Maloy, "History of Morris County - 1820 to 1890." pg. 65

[5] - Council Grove (KS) Democrat - October 31, 1872

Chapter 17
The Town-Builder

America began moving west at a rapid pace, once the War Between The States was brought to a close. The Missouri, Kansas & Texas Railroad was built down the Neosho River valley and played a great part in the development of the area, including Charles G. Parker's town of Parkerville.

The M.K. & T. Railroad actually started out as an entirely different line. In the spring of 1863, congress passed legislation which was intended to link the military posts of the Midwest together by rail. Already the advantage of rail travel was obvious and the military was quick to use the idea. Consequently, in February of 1865, a railroad called the Union Pacific, Southern Branch, was chartered. It's intended route was south from Fort Riley into the Clark's Creek valley, then into the Neosho River valley, following that to the point where it crossed into Indian Territory, now Oklahoma. From that point, it had corporate rights to extend through Indian Territory to Ft. Gibson and Ft. Smith.[1]

A great amount of legal and financial gyrations took place in the next few years, but by 1870, the Missouri, Kansas & Texas Railroad had emerged when the dust had settled. The new railroad was quite a financial boon to the area. Hezekiah Brake, who had returned from Santa Fe and settled on Slough Creek northwest of Council Grove, wrote of his experience in providing ties for the road. He said, "Our native timber furnished the ties. I was to provide two hundred oak and walnut ones at seventy-five cents apiece. I employed four men at a dollar, and an overseer at a dollar and a quarter per day, and my ties were made, delivered and paid for, before spring. A Mr. Parker and a Mr. McKenzie[2] were pushing the grading[3] of the road, and it was carried forward with so much energy that by the spring of

---

[1] - Collias & George, "Katy Power," Crestwood, MO, 1986
[2] - This was Charles G. Parker and a neighbor, Lewis McKenzie, who would later serve several terms as a County Commissioner.
[3] - A community legend has it that Mr. Parker used some of the mules that he had used on the trail for this grading project on the railroad. It is unknown if this is true, but it seems unlikely.

1868, Council Grove had a good depot, and was a town on the new railroad. The rejoicing of the people was general, and many were the extravagant prophesies concerning the future prosperity of the town. But when Council Grove changed it's place as the great rendezvous of freighters over the Santa Fe Trail for a station on the (rail) road to Junction City, she bartered away much of her success as a town. However, it was pleasant to know that at last we were in touch with the State, the Nation, and the world at large."[1]

We can't know for sure that Charles G. Parker had planned this move all through the years, but in 1869 he hired a Mr. Reynolds to come and survey and plot out 71.48 acres of his claim into a town which was to be called Parkerville. The area was already acknowledged to be his territory as evidenced by an M. K. &T. timetable dated "effective October 1, 1870," indicating that the north bound train would arrive at "Parker's" at 6:15 PM and the south bound train would arrive at "Parker's" at 8:20 AM.[2]

Charles G. Parker now made his move. On February 18, 1871, Parkerville was officially incorporated as a city of the third class. The incorporators were Charles G. Parker, J. A. Rogers, G. W. Clark, H. Daniels, and W. M. Thomas, and these, by the articles of incorporation, were made the first trustees of the town. The next spring an election was held for town officers. At that election, J. W. Wallace was elected mayor.[3]

An interesting sidelight is that a post office had been established in the settlement under the name of "Parkersville" on August 9, 1870, with Charles G. Parker as the first post master. Although an earlier plat exists indicating the name of the town was to be "Parkersville,"[4] when it was incorporated, it was "Parkerville."

[1] - Hezekiah Brake, "On Two Continent - A Long Life's Experience", Self-published in 1896, Topeka, KS, Pg. 206
[2] - Council Grove (KS) Democrat - January 26, 1871
[3] - A. T. Andreas - "History of The State of Kansas," Chicago, 1883, pg. 808
[4] - My thanks to Ken McClintock of Council Grove who called my attention to the existence of this document. An interesting feature of that older, unused plat is that the street names are entirely different. For example, the present Pearl Street was called Pleasant Street and the present Main Street was called Market Street.

The name of the post office was finally changed to coincide with the name of the town on June 23, 1892.[1]

Very quickly, the little town began to take form. A reporter for the Junction City Union made a trip down the railroad that spring and gave this report.[2] –

"On a recent trip down the M. K. & T., we took the opportunity to stop a day at the prosperous little village of Parkerville, and were surprised at the improvements that have been and are now being made at that place. Six months ago, Mr. Wm. M. Thomas' store was one of the three buildings on the town site. It now contains thirty-five buildings and a population of about one hundred and fifty. Very few of our new railroad towns have grown faster, and we have seen none that have made more substantial improvements. Nearly all the buildings are quite large, and would be a credit to any place.

"Mr. Parker is erecting a first-class flouring mill, 30 x 40 feet, three stories high, which when completed will have a capacity of about two hundred and forty bushels of wheat per day. He has it nearly enclosed and expects to have it in operation by the time new wheat is ready for market. The mill will prove a great convenience to the farmers in the vicinity of Parkerville, and of immense benefit to the town.

"They have commenced the erection of a fine two-story stone school house, thirty feet square, which is to be furnished with the latest improved furniture and apparatus and will be an ornament and a blessing to the community. Mr. Hersam, whose wife is at present in the millinery business in this city, is putting up a stone building, 20 x 40 feet, two stories high, to be used as a store room and residence.

"Many other improvements are being made, but we had not time to ascertain particulars. Parkerville is doing more business than any town of its size in the state. It has some fifteen good, reliable business houses, representing nearly all classes of merchandise, but our space forbids our mentioning the names of the different firms.

"We learned that our conductor, G. H. Reynolds, and Mr. Olney, of Junction City, have purchased forty acres of land adjoining the town site, and have laid it out into lots and are selling them quite

---

[1] - Robert W. Baughman, "Kansas Post Offices," Topeka, KS, 1961, pg. 99
[2] - Junction City (KS) Union, June 24, 1871

rapidly. We were pleased to meet quite a number of Junction City folks who have located there. We heard it talked that they expect soon to give Council Grove a pretty close vote on the county seat question. All in all, we found Parkerville a real lively little village, and were much pleased with our visit."[1]

A view of early Parkerville, looking west up Railroad Avenue.
(*Author's Collection*)

As the reporter from Junction City revealed in his article, the idea emerged to petition for a county election to move the county seat to Parkerville. Perhaps it wasn't really a new idea, after all. A town legend has it that Charles G. Parker intended all along that the park, one city block right in the middle of town, should be the court house square.

---

[1] - My thanks to Loren Otis of White City for calling my attention to this interesting article about early Parkerville.

Chapter 18
The Battle For The Court House

Those strong, hardy souls that have had their lives consumed with the building of the towns of western America have always had the hope that their favorite burg would ultimately become a major metropolis. Not many did, but that was their dream.

In the early days of Kansas, battles for the county seat often turned bloody. The reasoning, of course, was that a town so designated was almost sure to survive and grow. With that success, would come monetary reward for those who had town lots to sell.

Prior to the founding of Parkerville, Council Grove was considered to be the county seat, simply because it was the only town in the county. It fact, it had been designated as such by the state legislative assembly when the county name was changed from Wise to Morris on Feb. 11, 1859.[1]

It is difficult to follow all of the actions involved during this tumultuous time. Parkerville was incorporated in February of 1871, and by July the county commissioners had been petitioned for an election to determine the location for the county seat. The question was simple - should it be in Council Grove or in Parkerville. On July 17, the petition was granted with the election set for September 6, and the contest was on. A check of the petition asking for the election was sought, and the petition was brought into question. On July 21st, the board of commissioners decided to rescind their action that called for a county seat election. Evidently, there was a considerable amount of behind-the-scenes politicking that night, and the next day the petition was re-sustained and the election was again ordered for September 6.[2]

Each town employed doubtful methods to get votes. Both towns offered good wages for temporary employment. Reports from numerous sources tell of laborers being brought in for a short period of time, simply for one more vote. It has been said that there were as many herders to be found surrounding each town as there were heads

---

[1] - Terr. L. 1859, Ch. 60, Sec. 1
[2] - Minutes, Vol. B, Pg. 109, 111 In Commissioners' Journal

of cattle. In Parkerville, men were hired to beautify the town. The city park in the center of town received much of their efforts.

In Council Grove, prior to the election, much work was done on the streets to keep laborers there until after the election. Gasoline lamps were installed at the street corners and a public bath house was built. At this time, the cemetery wall was laid up by the workers from afar.[1] Financing for these vote-getting projects was provided in some imaginative ways. One such project was a contest in which a glass toilet set was awarded to the most popular woman in Council Grove. Mrs. Porter, a school teacher, and Miss Clara Ingram were the contestants, with Miss Ingram being the winner. It was said that this contest produced quite a sum for the building of the cemetery wall.[2] It can only be assumed that money produced votes in that contest, also.

This is not to suggest that dubious methods were used only by Council Grove. A. T. Andreas records one incident that may be representative of the activities of the whole contest. He says—

"People would come down from Parkerville to Council Grove and inveigle (definition- "To entice or to trick") away as many of the peripatetic (definition- "Moving from place to place") voters as possible, and, in like manner, the people of Council Grove would operate in Parkerville.

"On the night before the election a number laborers in Council Grove were thus enticed to go to Parkerville, and among them was one Irishman, who had been indulging rather freely in the "cratur." When they arrived at Parkerville, the descendent of Erin was taken to a hotel and assigned a room. Pat was not altogether reliable, for in his frequent potations he would give a whoop and "hoo-rooh" for Council Grove. After plying him with whisky, they undressed him and put him to bed, after which they left him, taking his clothes with them. About the time the matutinal rooster began to crow, Pat woke with a terrible thumping in the head. His mind was all confused, and it was a few minutes before he became sufficiently collected to comprehend the situation. He then got out of the bed and

---

[1] - John Maloy, "History Of Morris County - 1820 to 1890", pg. 67
[2] -Lalla Maloy Brigham, "The Story Of Council Grove On The Santa Fe Trail," 1921, pg. 50

began to look for his clothes, but they were gone. He looked under the bed, behind the door, behind the washstand, but not a stitch of them could he find. Pat, however, was a man of good natural resources, and inasmuch as someone had stolen his clothes, he could see no wrong in stealing somebody else's. Acting upon this principle, he stepped out into the hall in his nether garments, and as many of the bedroom doors were open, the weather being warm, he had no trouble in clothing himself. The hour was early and not a sound was heard in the whole house. Pat went his rounds, taking a pair of pants out of this room, a vest out of that, a coat out of another, a hat out of the next, and last a pair of boots, which he did not put on until he reached the street. It was nothing but a fair exchange, thought the son of Erin, and he had got the best of the bargain. He then started out on foot for Council Grove, a distance of about twelve miles, and on reaching town he met Mr. Nichols, the Street Commissioner, for whom he had been working, and to whom he told his experience, adding, "Be jabers, they thought to get me to vote for Parkerville, and though they trated me moighty dasent, as you may see, here I am to vote for Council Grove."[1]

Though evidently bloodshed was avoided, ill feelings between the two towns intensified by these questionable actions right up to election day. In the year of 1871, Morris county had a population of 2,225, but only men were eligible to vote. Records show 1,312 votes were cast, with Council Grove receiving 899 and Parkerville 413.[2]

In 1873, a second petition was circulated on the question but was rejected after a squabble over the names on the petition.[3] After that first election on September 6, 1871, this little item appeared in the Council Grove newspaper - "The county seat question has not killed our neighbor town, Parkerville, not even dampened the spirits of her people. Buildings are being erected every day, and business is brisk and on the increase. No town in the state, of it's age, can show a more energetic and persevering class of citizens. We wish them success."[4]

---

[1] - A. T. Andreas - "History Of The State Of Kansas," Chicago, 1883, pg. 802

[2] - Council Grove (KS) Republican, April 28, 1961

[3] - Minutes, Vol. C, Pg. 27-30 In Commissioners' Journal

[4] - Council Grove (KS) Democrat, November 2, 1871

As with all such contests, the ill feelings lingered long. A letter written by a Parkerville resident to the local paper on another subject, made this reference to Council Grove - "We cannot forget that the position they now occupy as county seat of the county was obtained through one of the most stupendous frauds ever perpetrated on a free and enlightened people."[1]

More than a century and a quarter have passed since the court house fight. Council Grove built a beautiful limestone building which served well for many years until a new court house fight broke out. This time, however, the lines were drawn between those who recognized the historical value of the old structure and those who wanted a modern building. The latter group won, and in the late 1960's, the old one was torn down, the stones hauled away, and a new building built in it's place.

So the long shadows of that early day battle between the two towns still linger, and questions about the election remain unanswered. Mrs. Frank Prescott, writing in a column called "Early Days in Ohio Township," in the Council Grove Republican of July 21, 1954, said, "Council Grove got the court house by fraud and Parkerville got the most beautiful park in the state."

The court house that might have been in Parkerville
(Courtesy Photography and Frame Shoppe)

---

[1] - Morris County Enterprise (Parkerville, KS) July 25, 1878

Chapter 19
The Neosho River Mill

For more than twenty-five years, the Parkerville business scene was dominated by the presence of the Neosho River Mill. It was being built in the spring of 1871 when that Junction City reporter made his trip to visit Parkerville.[1] He described it as being 30 by 40 feet in size, and three stories high. We know from other sources that it was a stone building. As originally built, the mill had four runs of burrs, and had a capacity of 120 barrels of flour every twenty-four hours.[2] It stood at the southwest corner of the town, south of the railroad tracks, between the town and the river.[3] In spite of it being situated near the river, it was a steam-driven mill and was used for sawing lumber as well as grinding grain. Unfortunately, no known photograph of the mill survives.

An item in a land abstract presents just a hint of a thought that possibly Charles G. Parker's brother, Henry, was involved in the mill project. A mortgage, dated September 26, 1872, indicates that Charles G. Parker borrowed $3,000 from Henry Parker who was living in St. Louis.[4] That was a lot of money in those days, but it was secured by as mortgage on eighty acres of prime Neosho valley land.

The 1870 St. Louis census lists Henry Parker as being 54 years old, four years older than Charles. He was married to 36-year old Mary, but no children were listed. Henry's occupation was listed as "keeps saw mill" and Mary's as "keeps house." An interesting detail of that census form is that there was a column to list value of real estate and value of personal estate. Henry's real estate is listed at $60,000 and his personal estate at $50,000. Mary's real estate was given as $16,000 and her personal estate at $13,000. No other individual's wealth listed on that form comes close to approaching

---

[1] - Junction City (KS) Union, June 24, 1871.
[2] - A. T. Andreas - "History Of The State Of Kansas," Chicago, 1883, pg. 809
[3] - Interview with Lee Haun, owner of the mill site - 1996
[4] - Land Abstract - Author's Collection

70

theirs, with the next highest listed at $3,000 real estate and $800 personal estate.[1]

Perhaps the scenario went something like this - Charles had spent all of his ready cash buying up real estate and in the process of finishing up the financing of his new mill, he found himself strapped for funds. A letter to St. Louis to brother Henry explaining his situation found a sympathetic ear. Henry knew that there was money to be made with a mill, so he was ready to invest. Being a shrewd businessman, however, he thought that a mortgage on some of that beautiful land would be a good idea.

Again, we're only guessing as to the use of those funds borrowed from brother Henry. However, the mortgage was not paid off until Henry's death in December of 1888.

It is impossible to compile any kind of a true history of the mill for lack of information. However, after the first newspaper in Parkerville began publication in January, 1878, occasional items appeared that give somewhat of a running account of the activity of the local industry. Without footnotes referencing the newspaper names, as there was never more than one paper in town at a time, here are some of the news items about the mill.

Jan. 24, 1878 - NEOSHO VALLEY MILLS (The name seemed to shift around) Mr. J. T. Girard, who formerly conducted the milling business at this place, has returned to take charge of the mill again. His reputation as a first-class and practical miller is too well established to need any comment at our hands. He purposes putting the mill in good repair, and will be prepared to accommodate his customers promptly.

April 5, 1878 - Mr. J. T. Girard having left the mill at this place, Mr. Parker has secured the services of Mr. Stone to conduct the business. Mr. Stone was the first miller at Parkerville.

August 29, 1878 - The Neosho Mills are now kept constantly busy grinding. They turn out some of the best flour manufactured in the state.

---

[1] - My thanks to the Missouri Historical Society, St. Louis, for this information.

71

May 15, 1879 - The atmosphere around the mill in this place ought to be improved by all means. The wind coming up from that direction is laden with very disagreeable odors. On the principle that the hair of the dog will cure the bite, perhaps a few more pig pens erected in the rear of that establishment might abate the stench.

September 11, 1879 - The smoke stack on the mill at this place took a tumble last Saturday, thereby causing a suspension of work for a few days.

April 7, 1881 - C. G. Parker, proprietor of the mill at this place, has purchased during the past two weeks, between six and seven hundred bushels of wheat for which he has paid from 75 to 81 cents per bushel. He will make this into first-class flour for the home market.

January 2, 1882 - The mill at this place is kept constantly going, either grinding or sawing.

September 7, 1882 - When business hours arrived last Monday morning, it was found that both the miller, G. W. Wright, and the engineer, P. Harman and family, had quietly folded their tents and skipped out between two days. They did not, however, skip together, as Harman started for Council Grove by wagon, but was overtaken by parties who held a mortgage on his goods and made to disgorge, while Wright went to the Grove by train to join them, but he was met by an officer and made to settle up some business matters, after which he took the noon train for Emporia where he was to meet Harman's family, which contains a young girl with whom Wright had become very familiar, and proceed from there to New York. Wright has a wife and one child living at Enterprise, this state.

November 15, 1883 - Mr. C. G. Parker has again commenced work at the mill after a layoff of a week, during which time they were employed mending up the boiler. They are now prepared to do better work than ever.

August 8, 1884 - The Neosho Mills at this place, which have been shut down for some time, opened up last Friday. Whether it is intended to run the mill continually, we are unable to say.

March 10, 1888 - The firm of Wright & McKenzie has been dissolved, and the Neosho River Mills have been turned over to C. G. Parker. The move is the result of a scarcity of wheat in the neighborhood, the mill having used up all that could be procured. Mr. Parker will run the mill occasionally, as often as enough grain can be procured to justify the expense. Mr. Wright will be on hand, as formerly, to receive grain, paying the highest market price.

January 4, 1897 - The Parkerville mill sent another load of meal to Council Grove this week. Where once introduced, their meal takes the lead over all.

September 9, 1897 - The Parkerville mill will soon be a thing of the past as it is being torn down and will be shipped to Alva, Okla. It is too bad to have it removed, but we wish the proprietors success in their new field.

September 16, 1897 - A. N. Miller and family left Tuesday for Alva, Okla., where Mr. Miller has moved the mill.

The Neosho River Mill had served it's purpose. At one time drawing business from many miles away as the country filled up with the land seekers from afar, it was now obsolete and unprofitable to operate. Charles G. Parker, now nearly eighty years old, was out of the milling business. The mill was thus consigned to history.

Chapter 20
A Love Grown Cold

When Charles G. Parker was contemplating the state of holy matrimony back in the spring of 1867, it is possible that he experienced a few apprehensive thoughts about the matter. After all, Charlottie (the name also appears Charlotte and Charlotty) was less than half his age. Those many trips across the plains to Santa Fe may have taken a toll on his physical condition and he might have looked even older than he really was. Perhaps her earlier marriage was a bit of a question mark to him. Maybe he never really knew what caused it to end.

No photographs of Charlottie are known to exist, but we might imagine that she was quite lovely. We can only guess about that, but we can be sure that she was a free-spirited young lady from existing evidence in regards to her relationship with a local church.

Several of the families in the valley in the Parkerville area had traveled down river about 8 miles to the Morris School House where they organized the Neosho Valley Union Baptist Church. The first meeting, presided over by Elder Ezra Johnson, was held there on October 26, 1865. As most of those families, the names including Burton, Kendall, Ramsey, Cress and others, lived within a mile or two of Parkerville, the congregation had moved to Parkerville by September of 1867. There they met in a small log school house south of the river called the Black School. Charlottie Parker, at some unrecorded date, joined that little Baptist Church on the basis of "experience and baptism."

On Saturday before the second Sabbath in January of 1871, at a business meeting of the church, "after the peace of the church was called for, all at peace," the case of Sister Charlottie Parker was brought up. She was charged with "going to balls and dancing." A committee, consisting of Sisters Nancy Cress and Sarah Blackburn, was appointed to visit her and report back at the next regular business meeting.

At the following business meeting in February of 1871, the report of the committee was deferred until the next regular meeting. It was a full year before the minutes of another business meeting were recorded. Nothing more is mentioned about Charlottie, but next to her name on the membership list is written the word, "Excluded." The wife of the town founder had been "churched out."[1]

No information exists to suggest that Charles G. Parker was even a bit troubled about his wife's problems with the church. He may have even found it a bit amusing, as he had never shown any interest in spiritual matters. Besides, he was busy with the formation of his new town and getting ready for the county seat election.

After the disappointment of that failed race for the court house, the life of Charles and Charlottie Parker probably settled into a routine of work and social events. The mill would have taken much of his time, along with the farm, which he may have rented out. A couple of embarrassing law suits were brought in district court against him[2], but they were probably brought to a conclusion without too much difficulty.

The social whirl of the little town kept everyone busy. Notice of a Thanksgiving ball was printed in the county seat newspaper, stating "our neighbors at Parkerville are preparing to give a grand ball at that place on the evening of Thanksgiving Day. Every arrangement will be made to make it an agreeable affair. Good music has been secured and a large attendance is expected. We predict that it will be a grand affair, as the people of that burg do nothing by halves. Of course, Council Grove will go up en masse and give tone to the occasion. Success to the efforts of our Parkerville friends who desire to furnish social amusement to their fellow mortals."[3] Apparently the arrangements for the social event weren't quite complete, as the next issue carried the news that "The Parkerville people have postponed their ball until about Christmas."[4]

In the spring of 1873, activities around town were many and varied. The Council Grove Democrat sent a reporter up the river to

---

[1] - This material about the Neosho Valley Union Baptist Church is from the original clerk's book which was in the possession of Mrs. Priscilla Moore, who allowed this writer to copy the material prior to her death. The Parkerville Baptist Church is the outgrowth of that little work that began in 1865.

[2] - Council Grove (KS) Democrat, October 31 and Nov. 7, 1872.

[3] - Ibid., November 21, 1872

[4] - Ibid., November 28, 1872

check on the situation and he wrote an article that gave mixed reviews to the town. Among other things he said, "The people there are stirring in local matters, and are industriously making up a coal company, to the capital stock of which the people are subscribing liberally. Boring will commence at once, as the leases have all been secured. Politics are assuming a threatening aspect—we mean town politics—as the line will be drawn between the dancing and the non-dancing denizens. Business is dull, but on the improvement."[1]

He concluded his thoughts with this statement - "Parkerville is a clever little town. We like the people. We like the country around about it. Nothing but county seat contests ever mar our pleasant intercourse."[2]

The summer of 1873 was probably busy with the preparations for an agricultural fair that was held on October 17th. Viewed from down the river, the opinion was "Our Parkerville friends deserve all credit for inaugurating and conducting the first annual fair of Morris County."[3]

That winter there was a time of religious revival in the community. "Our Parkerville friends are being blessed with a great revival of religion. Some twenty converts have been baptized. It is the joint work of the Baptists and Methodists," was the published report.[4] It would be interesting to know if Charlottie attended any of these meetings. It seems unlikely.

The spring of 1874 saw continued prosperity in the vicinity. Another long item published in the county seat newspaper about the town concluded with this thought - "Parkerville is a good place to go."[5]

It may have seemed so on the surface, but to those that were "in the know," it was a different story. Without doubt, there were those in the vicinity who were not at all surprised when the word was passed all through the village that, after seven years of marriage, Charles G. Parker, now fifty-four years old, had sued thirty year old Charlottie for divorce. Perhaps some of the neighbors were taken by

---

[1] - Council Grove (KS) Democrat, March 4, 1873

[2] - Ibid.

[3] - Ibid. October 21, 1873

[4] - Ibid. December 16, 1873

[5] - Ibid. March 24, 1874

surprise by the action, but no doubt, others were aware of problems in the marriage and with Charlottie's conduct. Maybe someone even said, "The Baptists knew what they were doing, all along."

The trip to the county seat must have been a painful one for Charles G. Parker as he contemplated filing for divorce. He evidently had stopped by the office of Sharp & McDonald to secure their services. Their offices were upstairs over the First National Bank on Main Street.[1] As he told his story, notes were taken and when the petition was filed, it contained this sad account –"On or about the 26th day of March, A. D. 1866, at Clarks Creek, in the County of Morris, and State of Kansas, he was married to the defendant; and he has ever since conducted himself towards the said Charlottie Parker as by his marital contract he agreed to do.

"The defendant, regardless of her marital duties, on the 19th day of August, A. D. 1874, at the house occupied by said defendant and one (name withheld) as a ladies' dress-making shop, in the city of Parkerville, and county of Morris, and state of Kansas, did commit adultery with one (her business partner's husband - name withheld).

"The defendant, regardless of her marital duties, has for more than one year past, wholly and grossly neglected her domestic and household duties.

"The plaintiff prays that he may be divorced from the said Charlottie Parker and that he may have such other and further relief as equity may require." The petition was dated August 31, 1874.[2]

We can never know all that went into negotiations following that action, but an effort was made to reconcile the problems. An undated document accompanying the divorce papers carries this message - "By consent of parties, it is agreed that the above initiated action be dismissed at the cost of plaintiff." The divorce was cancelled.

Perhaps coincidentally, the Council Grove Democrat carried a little item in December of 1875 that "the other man" had left Parkerville for Maine, "where his business interests demand his presence."

---

[1] - Business Directory, Council Grove Democrat, April 14, 1874
[2] - Archives, Clerk of the District Court, Council Grove, KS

77

Chapter 21
Love Grown Cold - Part 2

With the dismissal of the divorce action, Charles G. Parker and his young wife, Charlottie, probably sat down at the kitchen table in that big stone house in Parkerville and talked about their future. We might imagine that there were appropriate apologies from Charlottie for her wayward conduct, if she was really guilty of it all. Maybe she even insisted that it was all a mistake. One way or the other, they sat about to rebuild their marriage, but it just didn't work out.

So one more time, Charles G. Parker found his way to a lawyer's office, this time to the partnership of Bradley & Nicholson. The petition was filed on February 24, 1876, just eighteen months after the first divorce action was filed. Again, he told his sad story while they took notes. Again, proper papers were filed, petitioning for divorce. Things were much more serious this time, though.

--"The defendant has abandoned the plaintiff for more than one year before the commencement of this action, and has been willfully absent from the plaintiff during that time.

--"That in the summer of 1870, at Parkerville, County of Morris and State of Kansas, the said defendant willfully, unlawfully and in violation of her marriage vows and obligations, committed adultery with one (name withheld).

--"That in the winter of 1869-70, at Junction City, County of Davis, and State of Kansas, the defendant willfully, unlawfully and in violation of her marriage vows and obligations committed adultery with one (name withheld).

--"That in the month of July, 1873, at Parkerville, county of Morris and State aforesaid, the defendant willfully, unlawfully and in violations of her marriage vows and obligations, committed adultery with one (name withheld, but one of the other town founders) and at divers times before and since said July 1873, and at various places in said County of Morris and State aforesaid, committed adultery with the said (same man).

--"That at various times and in various places in the State of Kansas and in the State of California, before and since the abandonment of the plaintiff by the defendant as aforesaid, the defendant has committed adultery with divers parties to this plaintiff unknown."

The sad story boiled down to this, she was either a woman with very loose morals or she was a very unfortunate young woman married to a very jealous old man. Either way, because of circumstances, she had fled to California within six months of the filing of that first divorce petition in August of 1874.

The paperwork kept the lawyers busy as the action proceeded. Charlottie responded that she couldn't be present at the trial because she had no money and was sick and could not work. Her answer, prepared by her local attorney, A. Moser, Jr., also made some interesting allegations. She said—

--"That in spite of his marital duties and obligations toward me, had been guilty of adultery at various times, to wit, at Topeka, Kansas, on or about the 7th day of September, 1873, with a woman whose name is unknown to this defendant, and at Parkerville, Morris County, Kansas, on or about the __ of February and March 1875 with one (name withheld). And at various times within the last year at Parkerville in said County with one (name withheld)."

James Fletcher Cress, having been duly sworn, said that "he is the agent for the plaintiff who is at the present time in the State of California, that he has read the foregoing answer and crossbill for divorce and he says the allegations therein contained are true as he verily believes."

Charles G. Parker, through his attorney, said that "he has paid the defendant twenty-five dollars as, and for, attorney's fees and forty-two dollars other alimony and that this affiant has not been able, by reason of his poverty, to pay said defendant any other or further sum as required by this court."

The whole neighborhood was getting into the mess. Samuel Sanford Jr. swore that he was well acquainted with Charles G. Parker's finances and he estimated him to be worth $20,000. J. J. Thomas, being duly sworn, said that he had been in the real estate business in Morris County for more than five years. He said that Charles G. Parker owned a farm worth $8,000, a steam mill and a large stone house of the value of about $10,000, various vacant lots, and a one-half interest in a two story stone store building worth $800. His statement was signed on September 4, 1876.

By way of her physician, Dr. J. A. Burns, the court was notified that Charlottie, living in the city of Sacramento, CA, was not well, indicating "that her ailment is of such a nature afflicting her internally." He also said "That her health and physical condition is such as to render it highly improper and even hazardous for her to travel from here to the state of Kansas, or even to travel at all."

On the 4th day of September, 1876, F. L. Parker, brother of Charlottie, came before the court to swear that her health had been bad since February of that year, prohibiting her from supporting herself by working and that she had called on him for financial help. The judge signed an order that day, delaying the trial until the next term of court, with temporary alimony of six dollars per week.

The following April, H. E. Richter, Sheriff of Morris County, served papers on more than a dozen of the Parkerville neighbors to appear as witnesses at the divorce trial which was to take place that month. From the remaining documents, it is impossible to know what all took place, either in or out of the court room. Obviously factors came into play that are not recorded in official court papers, but we do have one document that brings the case to a conclusion for us.

"Chas. G. Parker vs. Charlotte Parker, Case dismissed. And now May 2, 1877, comes the plaintiff by his attorney and also comes the defendant by her attorney and the plaintiff asks leave to dismiss his petition without prejudice and the defendant also asks leave of the court to dismiss her answer and cross bill without prejudice which is granted, and it is ordered that this case be dismissed without prejudice and that the costs herein be taxed to the plaintiff and for the same execute a May issue."[1]

Notice was made of the disposition of the case in the county seat newspaper with this small item, "C. G. Parker vs. Charlottie Parker, dismissed at cost of plaintiff."[2] The community probably breathed a collective sigh of relief with that news, but there are questions that still remain unanswered. Nothing in the court

---

[1] - Archives, Clerk of the District Court, Council Grove, KS
[2] - Council Grove (KS) Democrat, May 17, 1877

documents reveals if Charlottie returned for the trial in May of 1877. We don't know if there was a reconciliation between the two parties or not, nor do we know if they ever returned to that big stone house where they spent the early years of their marriage.

Exactly five months to the day after that divorce case was dismissed, Charlotte Parker was dead. A search of all area newspapers has failed to produce even a notice of her death, much less an obituary. Nothing is known about that internal illness spoken of by her doctor in California, but it may have been what killed her. The only certainty is that she is buried in the Ramsey-Black Cemetery about half a mile east of Parkerville. Her tombstone reads:

Charlotty, Wife of C. G. Parker

Died Nov. 2, 1877

33 years, 9 months, 2 days

The headstone at Charlottie Parker's grave in the Ramsey-Black Cemetery east of Parkerville. (*Author's Collection*)

Chapter 22
Community Criticism

With the passage of more than one hundred and twenty years, it is difficult to determine the community's attitude toward the divorce drama and the ultimate death of Charlottie Parker. Probably, as with most situations, there were two sides to the matter, and it is possible that the community chose up sides.

A single item appeared in the county seat newspaper that would lead us to believe that Charles G. Parker found himself under a blanket of criticism in his own town. One of the interesting aspects of the item is that it is on an entirely different subject. After a severe early winter storm in the fall of 1877, one of his neighbors wrote this letter to the editor. It appeared in print just eight days after Charlottie's death.[1]

"Editors, Republican and Democrat;

Mr. C. G. Parker of this place has recently had the misfortune to lose several very fine hogs. Their death has been attributed by some to hog cholera and by others to eating too much salt, Mr. Parker having fed them rather plentifully of salt a day or two previously. Others still think their death was caused by exposure to the cold storm of last week. During the first of the storm, the hogs, some forty to fifty in number, were kept in a rather small enclosure which soon became, as one might say, swimming in mud and filth, but before the storm, which lasted several days, was over, Mr. Parker succeeded in getting a plank floor to his pen. The floor was of green elm or oak, with no roof to protect the hogs from the rain, and the siding, merely a common board fence, opposed no obstacle to the wind sweeping through. The hogs were in this condition when the disease first took hold of them. In two or three days, sixteen out of the seventeen attacked died. The one is in a fair way to recover. There are no new cases and the disease seems to have abated. It is of exceeding interest to farmers to know whether the hogs died of cholera, and also whether they died of eating salt or exposure. There are certain known remedies for the latter two, the one not to feed too much salt, the other

---

[1] - Council Grove (KS) Republican & Democrat - November 10, 1877

to provide suitable protection for the hogs.   There is criminal carelessness all through the county in furnishing protection to stock, and particularly hogs. Farmers better look to your interests.

L.B.

Parkerville, Kansas

No doubt, Mr. Parker knew which one of his neighbors had the initials of L. B. It seems likely that the writer intended it that way. Although the letter was written on the subject of hogs, perhaps the intended message was simply that Charles G. Parker failed to care for those precious things of life, whether it be a wife or livestock. Who knows what was in the mind of the writer. It does seem strange, though, that a letter written in such a manner would appear so soon after the death of his wife.

Chapter 23
Life Moves On

After the death of Charlottie, Charles G. Parker entered into the activities of his town with a new enthusiasm. The spring of 1878 saw the first newspaper ever printed in Parkerville begin it's weekly appearance. David O. McCray was the editor. It was named "Morris County Enterprise," and carried the slogan, "A paper for the people of Morris County." A listing of the local businesses was carried in that first edition and it included "NEOSHO MILLS owned by Mr. C. G. Parker. It is one of the best mills on the Neosho River, and has a splendid patronage. Mr. Parker is a clever gentleman and is the founder of Parkerville."[1]

Week by week, the Enterprise chronicled events and expressed opinions that the readers may have agreed with or disagreed with, without concern to the editor. In several issues the editor announced, "We will take wood or any kind of farm produce on subscriptions to the Enterprise. Gold, silver, or greenbacks not refused."

It was in the pages of the Enterprise that the name of the next Mrs. Parker first appeared in a rather innocent fashion. "Miss Mattie Fall will please accept the thanks of Mrs. McCray for a beautiful bouquet."[2] It would be several years before she would take on that new title, though.

Meanwhile, many social activities were taking place in the little town that must have kept Charles G. Parker busy. "There will be a Grand Ball at Parker's Hall in Parkerville, under the auspices of Quilhot & Drake (local businessmen) on the evening of July 4th, 1878. A magnificent time is anticipated. Great pains will be taken by these gentlemen to maintain the best of order. Tickets 50 cents. Dancing will commence at 8 o'clock p.m. All lovers of dancing are cordially invited."[3]

---

[1] - Morris County Enterprise, Parkerville, KS, January 3, 1878
[2] - Ibid., May 23, 1878
[3] - Ibid., June 27, 1878

The Morris County Enterprise also recorded the week by week details of an illness that nearly took the old freighter's life. First notice of this came in the October 20, 1881, issue with this simple statement, "C. G. Parker is suffering from an attack of pneumonia." The following week this item appeared - "C. G. Parker, spoken of last week as being afflicted with pneumonia, is now lying very low, the disease having assumed a typhoid form."

The issue of the following week (Nov. 3, 1881) carried the good news, "C. G. Parker is improving slowly and hopes are now entertained for his recovery." In the same issue appears this item - "A brother of C. G. Parker, from St. Louis, has been in the city since Tuesday, called hither by the severe illness of Mr. Parker." This, no doubt, was Henry S. Parker, spoken of in an earlier chapter. The next issue concluded the matter with this good news, "C. G. Parker is rapidly regaining strength."[1]

It was time for Charles G. Parker to make another visit to the county court house, certainly a more joyful occasion than other recent ones. So on the 19th of January, 1882, he and his new beloved, Mattie Fall (it also sometimes appears "Falls") went down to the county seat to secure a marriage license.[2] The Probate Judge could tell that the couple was old enough to marry, so he left their ages off the license. However, we know that Charles G. Parker was sixty-two and Mattie was fifty-two at this time. The local editor noted, "We are informed that there is to be another wedding in the city Sunday next."[3] However, he failed to carry any report of the ceremony itself.

The couple appeared before Rev. George A. Irvin, Pastor of the local Presbyterian congregation, on Sunday, January 29, 1882, and were joined in holy matrimony. The new Mrs. Parker was soon settled into that big stone house. During those years of his marriage to Mattie, Charles G. Parker probably enjoyed the most stable period of his long life. And very soon after his marriage to Mattie, a new dimension was added to his life—he became a church-going man.

In addition to the work being done in the community by the Baptists, the Methodists, and the Catholics, the Presbyterian

---

[1] - Morris County Enterprise, Parkerville, KS - Nov. 10, 1881
[2] - Archives, Clerk of the District Court, Council Grove, KS
[3] - Morris County Enterprise, Parkerville, KS - January 26, 1882

congregation had been active for some time. In January of 1882, they had adopted a plan to raise funds to put up a building.[1] Shortly after the Parker wedding, this announcement appeared in the local paper,[2] "Our Presbyterian friends will hold their next social at the school house in this city next Thursday evening. The money so raised is to be used in the building of a church edifice in this city, and the admission (only 10 cents) makes it within the reach of all to attend."

It must have been a discouraging place to minister for the Rev. Irvin. The town was not particularly spiritual, even with all of the religious efforts being put forth. Consequently, several factors may have gone into his decision that was announced in this manner - "Rev. G. A. Irvin has given up his ministerial labors at this point. He has labored faithfully at this point for a number of years and will be sadly missed by his many friends and admirers who regret deeply that the state of his health compels him to pursue this course."[3]

With Rev. Bicknell as their new pastor, the congregation was still seeking to get their building constructed. Consequently, in June of 1884, they held a meeting, which was reported like this - "The Presbyterian friends at their meeting last Thursday elected as their board of trustees, H. S. Day, B. Kinner, Jos. Noggle, C. G. Parker and Dr. Hopkins. They have something like $600 already subscribed for the building of their church, and the committee has done but little soliciting so far. We have seen the plan of the church building and must say that it is to be the neatest church that has so far been built in our county, and will cost from $2,500 to $3,000."[4]

No doubt this meeting was seen by the congregation as a great step forward. These men were all prosperous men in the community and would serve, not only with their wisdom, but also with their finances. Little did they know that it was, in fact, the death knell for this church. Not many months down the road a family feud would break out between H. S. Day and Dr. James Hopkins. It would go on for some time, coming to a tragic conclusion in the shooting of Dr. Hopkins by H. S. Day.[5] This event seemed to close the book on the

---

[1] - Morris County Enterprise, Parkerville, KS - January 12, 1882
[2] - Ibid. - February 16, 1882
[3] - Ibid. - October 12, 1882
[4] - Ibid. - June 20, 1884
[5] - Parkerville (KS) Times, October 22, 1887

Presbyterian Church. No building was ever built and very shortly all activity seemed to cease. When Charles G. Parker passed away in 1909, one line in his obituary reached back to this time in his life like this, "In earlier life he was a member of the Presbyterian Church."[1]

Charles G. Parker - The Founder Of Parkerville
(Courtesy Lee Haun)

---

[1] - Council Grove (KS) Guard - September 17, 1909

Chapter 24
The Golden Years

Charles G. Parker must have enjoyed great satisfaction as he looked out across his town. It had experienced considerable growth, at one point reaching a population of more than two hundred hardy pioneers.[1] Business was brisk, with such firms as N. Dilley & Co., bringing in customers from a great area   One honor had been bestowed on him some years earlier that may have given him special pleasure. As the county grew in population, it became necessary to create additional townships, for governmental purposes. Some area was taken from Neosho township and some from Clark's Creek township to form a new township. This township was established on September 5, 1870, and was named "Parker Township."[2]

The needs of those early pioneer were really quite limited. Shelter was always a necessity, as was food. These could be provided with a little effort by most people. One other necessity in the cold winter months was the need for a source of heat. With Parkerville situated in the timber belt along the Neosho River, many wood-burning stoves were kept hot night and day. A constant supply of wood demanded a great amount of time as well as a lot of hard work, however. Because of those factors, much more coal was burned in Parkerville and other towns in those early days than we might imagine.

Nearly every community hoped to discover a source of coal near by. Not only would it provide ready fuel, but also income for the area.   Efforts had been made in the Council Grove area without success.[3] A corporation was formed in the Parkerville area for that purpose also, but little is known about any activities by them.

Charles G. Parker felt the same need for coal, and perhaps for the income it would produce. His efforts were recorded like this - "DIGGING FOR COAL - C. G. Parker has for some time felt confident of the existence of coal on his farm and has at last

---

[1] - Kansas State Historical Society Research Center files
[2] - A. T. Andreas, "History of The State Of Kansas", Chicago, 1893, pg. 802
[3] - Council Grove (KS) Democrat, January 18, 1872

determined to unearth it. He has procured the services of an experienced miner and two assistants, who commenced work Tuesday. They are now down about twenty feet and are confident that within the next thirty feet they will strike a good vein of coal. Already they have passed through the gravel deposits usually found some distance above coal, and are now in the greenish soapstone, which is considered an excellent indication. Naturally, everybody in the vicinity is anxiously awaiting the result of this mining venture, and trusts that Mr. Parker's fondest hopes will be realized, as it will not only be a bonanza for him, but will also give Parkerville an importance second to no town in the county."[1] Three weeks later it was reported that a small vein of coal had been struck by the miners and that indications were that a larger vein would be found before long.[2] We can only guess that the larger vein was never found, and the miners went on to other places to dig for coal. They received no additional mention in the local paper.

Those were good years for Charles and Mattie Parker. He had probably achieved a position of respect in the community that had been lacking during those years that he and Charlottie were having difficulties. It wasn't uncommon for notices of social activities to appear in local papers. The big stone house on the west side of town was the place where Anna Lindsey Hopkins, only nineteen years old when she was widowed, married her second husband.

When her first husband, Dr. James Hopkins, was shot by the Mayor, H. S. Day, there were those in town that weren't really surprised. He seemed to be a bit of a ladies man, and that was bound to cause trouble. Now, however, she was marrying James Henderson Burton, a young man from one of the solid families in the community. Elder Ezra Johnson performed the ceremony on December 20, 1888. Only a few guests were present but later in the evening about forty of the groom's friends called and paid their respects by giving him a free ride in a carriage which they drew by hand. They traveled all over the village to the music of cow bells, tin horns and tin pans.[3]

---

[1] - Parkerville (KS) Times, March 31, 1888
[2] - Parkerville (KS) Times, April 21, 1888
[3] - White City (KS) News, December 28, 1888

Other events which were not as boisterous also occurred there. One was recorded like this - "LAWN SOCIAL - Mrs. C. G. Parker, of Parkerville, gave a very pleasant social last Saturday, in honor of Miss Jessie Parker and Miss Emma Sims, of Council Grove, who were visiting in Parkerville. There was a large and select attendance and the guests passed a very enjoyable time. Mrs. Parker is one of the best entertainers in the county and knows well how to make a company feel at home and enjoy themselves. Among the guests present we noticed the following: Miss Parker, Miss Emma Simms, W. R. McGeorge and Chas. Hamner, of Council Grove; J. E. Edgerton and wife and Mrs. Swetman, of White City, and the many friends of the hostess from Parkerville and vicinity."[1]

---

[1] - Council Grove (KS) Alliance Herald-Guard, July 24, 1891

Chapter 25
Trouble With The Law

In spite of the measure of respectability that he had gained with the passage of time, probably no one in the Parkerville area was surprised to learn that Charles G. Parker was in trouble with the law in regards to liquor. Most everyone in town was aware that he kept an assorted store of spirits on hand for his own use and for guests that might come by. Town legend has it that there were certain rooms in that big stone house that ladies were not allowed to enter. It was in those rooms that his supply of liquor was kept. Evidently, he never felt the need to secure the proper license to sell the liquor, perhaps on the pretense that he only gave it away.

We might imagine how his wife, Mattie, felt when the sheriff of Morris County showed up at her door on the evening of July 3, 1899. In his hand was a warrant for the arrest of her 79 year old husband, Charles G. Parker. He was accused of "The offense of unlawfully and without taking out and having a permit to sell intoxicating liquors, according to law, keeping and maintaining a place and places, where spirituous, vinous, malt, fermented, and other intoxicating liquors were sold in violation of law, to wit: In the building, buildings, dwelling houses, cellars, outhouses, barns, stables, groves, thickets, brush and other places situated on and about the northwest quarter of section 9, township fifteen, range 7, Morris County, State of Kansas, to the common nuisance of the good people of the state of Kansas, and especially to the common nuisance of the good people of the town of Parkerville and vicinity, and of the County of Morris, State of Kansas.

"And further that you do forthwith seize and take into your custody any and all property, intoxicating liquors and vessels and bottles containing the same, and all bar fixtures and paraphernalia belonging there to, herein before described which you may find in the possession of said Charles G. Parker."[1]

Arrested as a common boot-legger, the founder of the town could only stand by and watch as the sheriff searched his property, all

---

[1] - Archives, Clerk of the District Court, Council Grove, KS

the way from the "dwelling" to the "outhouse" and carried off his store of liquor. The county seat newspaper made this rather irreverent comment a few days later,[1] "Thirty-six cases of beer which were shipped to Parkerville for irrigating purposes on the 4th were "levied upon" by the sheriff on the evening of the 3rd. The town was exceedingly dry on the 4th."

Charles G. Parker had to call on a couple of his prosperous neighbors to help him out of this little difficulty. Down the river road they went on July 5, 1899, to that court house in Council Grove. There, along with Charles G. Parker, those neighbors, John Tague and T. W. Whiting, signed a five hundred dollar recognizance bond guaranteeing his appearance when the court date was set.[2]

When the sheriff wrote out his report on the raid on July 26, 1899, he said that he "found the following property - 34 cases of beer, supposed to contain 24 bottles each and one case partly empty and two cases of empty bottles, making in all 37 cases which I took into my possession and now hold subject to the order of the said court and have released the said Chas. G. Parker, he having given good and sufficient bond for his appearance at the next term of the court."

County Attorney John Maloy had probably heard many complaints from the townspeople of Parkerville about the free flowing liquor at the Parker place. In response to that, he prepared what surely would have seemed like an iron clad case against that old rascal, Charles G. Parker. He was prepared to file nine counts, covering dates all the way from January 1, 1899, to July 3, 1899. He even included this wording "unlawfully sell, barter, and give away." That would surely cover all possibilities of defense.

The trial date was set for November 20, 1899, at the court house in Council Grove, but when the time arrived, Charles G. Parker was not in sight. His attorney, C. T. Phillips, a Parkerville neighbor who also served his community as an auctioneer, filed a motion for a continuance of the case, on the basis that "the said, C. G. Parker, defendant, is sick and unable to leave his home." He had in his hand a sworn statement by another Parkerville neighbor, Dr. W. T. Harvey,

---

[1] - Council Grove (KS) Republican, July 7, 1899
[2] - All material pertaining to this case is from the Archives, Clerk of the District Court, Council Grove, KS

who included these words, "I visited professionally the said C. G. Parker on the 19th and 20th day of November, 1899, and he, the said C. G. Parker, is sick and unable to leave his room without greatly endangering his life."

Apparently there wasn't much that could be done, so the trial was continued until the March 1900 term of court. Lawyer Phillips evidently thought that if this ploy worked once, it should be good for a second time. Consequently, he showed up in court with another affidavit signed by W. T. Harvey, MD, which read "The said C. G. Parker is sick and it would be dangerous to his life for him at this time to leave his room and go to Council Grove, Kansas."

The immediate response by County Attorney John Maloy is unknown. He knew Charles G. Parker well. Ten years earlier when he had written his history of Morris County[1] he had said this about him, "Mr. Parker is an active, well-preserved man of over seventy. He has as few enemies as any man could have without surrendering all his individuality. He is a genial, wholesouled gentleman."

Perhaps John Maloy remembered what he had said about the old Santa Fe freighter when he asked Judge O. L. Moore to dismiss all charges against Charles G. Parker. The judge approved and signed the order on March 23, 1900.

---

[1] - John Maloy, "History Of Morris County - 1820 to 1890", pg. 30

Chapter 26
Difficult Years

The years passed quickly for Charles G. Parker and his wife, Mattie, and soon the cold hand of death touched their comfortable abode. It was around Christmas time in 1904 when Mattie fell ill. Without doubt, Dr. W. T. Harvey was on the scene and that he did all he could for her, but to no avail. She passed away on December 29, 1904. The cause of death was listed as pneumonia. Her funeral was held at the home, as was the custom of the day, with the service conducted by Rev. S. Ream of White City.[1] She is buried in the cemetery on the west side of Parkerville. An interesting fact is that in the same paper that tells of her death, an item says, "C. G. Parker shipped a car (load) of cattle to Kansas City Monday." He was evidently still in fairly good health at that time.

Life was lonely for the old freighter so he began to look for a housekeeper. Records are silent as to how he conducted his search, perhaps through a classified advertisement in some big city newspaper. However it was accomplished, he was successful. The Parkerville correspondent to the county seat paper first mentioned her in this item in the October 13, 1905 issue[2], "C. G. Parker has a new housekeeper from somewhere in the east." This was followed with the following items on November 3, 1905, "C. G. Parker, better known as Uncle Charley, went to Council Grove last Wednesday and surprised his friends by bringing home a new Mrs. C. G. Parker. We offer our congratulations and may their lives be a blessing to those about them, and may their declining years be their best." Also, this item was included in the same issue...."The young people of this village and vicinity serenaded Mr. and Mrs. C. G. Parker Thursday night of last week."

Life was starting to get complicated for the old trail freighter when about two weeks later, on November 17, 1905, this item appeared, "C. G. Parker, wife and daughter were in Council Grove

---

[1] - Council Grove (KS) Republican, January 5, 1905
[2] - These four items are from the Council Grove (KS) Guard on the dates mentioned.

Wednesday of last week." The neighbors probably were watching this drama unfold before their very eyes, wondering what might be the next act. They didn't have to wait very long, because the December 22, 1905, issue brought this item, "Mrs. Charles Parker's mother came from Chicago last week to spend the winter with her."

At this point, Charles G. Parker must have been wondering what in the world he had gotten himself into. Probably there were days that he wished he was back in New Mexico chasing the Indians who had stolen his mules. Anything would be better than the mess that he found himself in presently. The only good thing about it all is that this new Mrs. Parker, whose name we know as Isabel, and the rest of her troupe would be gone in less than six months. We'll deal with the circumstances of that departure in a later chapter.

Old ways die hard sometimes, and before the summer of 1906 was history, Charles G. Parker found himself in trouble with the law again. Once more it had to do with liquor. His neighbors probably read the item in the county seat newspaper,[1] and said to themselves, "Won't he ever learn?" Here's what they read—

VIOLATES PROHIBITORY LAWS

"Charles G. Parker, a citizen near Parkerville, was arrested by County Sheriff Pitsenburger Saturday morning and with three cases of beer and some whiskey was brought to Council Grove. In Justice Sherfy's court, Parker plead guilty to the charge of selling intoxicating drinks and maintaining a nuisance and was given by the court a fine of $100 and thirty days imprisonment. He was also required to give a bond for $1,000 not to sell or give away any intoxicating drinks during the next two years.

Charley Parker is a man 86 years old. He located in this county, as near as we could find, in 1849 (this is incorrect) and was the founder of Parkerville."

---

[1] - Council Grove (KS) Republican, August 16, 1906

Chapter 27
Looking Back

In spite of the swift passing of time, Charles G. Parker apparently enjoyed good health for many years. Because of that, he was able to engage in activities usually considered the domain of much younger men. One such custom was making the trip to Kansas City with cattle that he was shipping to market. On one of these trips he was observed by a Kansas City newspaper reporter who interviewed him, no doubt because of his obvious advanced years. This interview was then carried by the local newspaper.[1]

WAS A TRAIL FREIGHTER

"The following from the Drovers Telegram of last Monday is concerning a well known Morris County man:

"C. G. Parker, of Parkerville, Kansas, 89 years old (actually 86 years old), a freighter over the Santa Fe Trail from where Kansas City now stands to the far southwest 58 years ago, rode all night last night on a freight train from his home, and landed at the yards this morning with a car load of cattle from his own farm.

"Mr. Parker followed the occupation of a freighter for over 20 years, and had many a fight with Indians. He was also a freighter during the war days, and had to "stand in" with both sides when he approached the Missouri and Kansas lines around Kansas City.

"For thirty-eight years, Mr. Parker has lived on his present farm. Two years ago his wife died, and as he has no children, he is compelled to keep a housekeeper on his present farm to look after his home. He is in the enjoyment of health, and was out about the yards today with other stockmen looking after his cattle.

"That old Santa Fe Trail," said Mr. Parker, "Well, I once knew it so well that I could travel it day or night without going astray. I knew every little creek that crossed it for 1,500 miles, and every crook and turn along it's tedious winding way across the plains. In those early days we had to travel in trains in order to guard against the Indians. Sometimes we got separated, and frequently they stole our teams. We would give chase, and occasionally they would hide

---

[1] - Council Grove (KS) Republican, November 22, 1906

from us, and show fight. I have had arrows sent after me many a time, but was never very badly injured by them."

"I think the idea that originated in Kansas City of having the old trail marked is a splendid one. It was certainly famous and ought to have a place in history. The thousands of caravans and millions of cattle that passed over it, made it a highway that was of more than ordinary importance. While my days are about over, still the very thought of those early times on the old trail seems to bring back the spark of youth."

"Kansas City and these immense packing houses and stock yards were unknown when I was a freighter. Steamboating was a big industry at that time. The river bank here was lined with boats, and freight was piled up everywhere. Great long wagon trains with mules attached wound out over these hills and disappeared from sight on the prairies every day in the year. It certainly was an inspiring sight."

# # # # #

We can almost imagine the old freighter standing there with misty eyes looking out across the growing city and remembering what used to be wide open spaces where the wagon trains assembled. No doubt he wished for "the good old days."

There are a couple of items that are of special interest to us in the interview. In speaking of the death of his wife two years ago, he is ignoring his marriage to Isabel. Though she had abandoned him, he is still legally married to her at this time. Also, in saying "he is compelled to keep a housekeeper on his present farm to look after his home," he would lead us to believe that he had another housekeeper in his employment at this time. If this is a valid assumption, it would be Rose Rennolds, whom we will meet a little later.

Chapter 28
Isabel And Company

After Mattie had died, Charles G. Parker was a lonely old man in a great big house and he needed help, so in some manner he advertised for a housekeeper. Isabel (we never do learn her previous surname) came from Chicago and no doubt recognized an opportunity to profit personally by taking advantage of an old man in his declining years. In the process, she demanded and received holy matrimony. When she discovered that he was still sharp enough to out-wit her, she bailed out on the whole matter, abandoning him in June of 1906.

Realizing that it was necessary to get legally detached from her, Charles G. Parker made another trip to the county seat. Calling on his old friend, attorney John Maloy, for assistance, he filed for divorce from Isabel on September 17, 1907. Rose Rennolds was probably hired on by now as housekeeper and he wanted to clear up the estate so it would be free to do with as he pleased.

The divorce petition tells the story of how Isabel had attempted to move in and take control of his life and property. It reads as follows—[1]

"C. G. Parker, Plaintiff vs. Isabel D. Parker, Defendant
"The plaintiff for this cause of action and petition against said defendant alleges:

"That he has resided continually in Morris County, State of Kansas for forty years, and is now and all along has been a bona fide resident of said County and State.

"That on the 25th day of October, AD 1905, plaintiff and defendant were duly and legally intermarried and now are husband and wife; and that plaintiff further alleges that ever since said marriage and as long as defendant lived with him, he conducted himself toward her in all respects as a faithful, affectionate and provident husband, but avers further that the said defendant, on the contrary, has been and is guilty of violating her marital vows, in this, to wit:

---

[1] - Archives, Clerk of the District Court, Council Grove, KS

"That defendant at first was employed by plaintiff, who was an old man, to keep house for him on his farm, near Parkerville in said Morris County, Kansas, and for that purpose only, but plaintiff avers that defendant soon came to him with the statement that she could not conscientiously remain unless she were married to plaintiff, but plaintiff refused to marry at the time, on account of his age and other potential reasons, but says that after defendant had procured the intercession of two or three neighboring women, he did at last consent, and the marriage took place as herein before alleged.

"Plaintiff further alleges that soon after said marriage, the temper and disposition of defendant changed for the worse, as plaintiff all along had feared; that defendant brought to plaintiff's house without his permission, a daughter, her mother, and a strange woman to do the cooking; and also had her son, about fifteen years of age (to come), not withstanding the fact that defendant was first hired and subsequently married for the sole purpose of becoming the cook and housekeeper for the two, plaintiff and defendant; that defendant came to plaintiff from Chicago, Ill., and brought the others above named from said city, also.

"Plaintiff further alleges that defendant's said boy was a stubborn, wild, unruly and incompatible lad, who paid no attention to plaintiff's rights and authority, and who roamed about the farm, constantly in mischief, and among other things willfully and wantonly shot two of plaintiff's mules, and on several occasions stole money from plaintiff; that although plaintiff was inclined not to murmur because of defendant's colonization upon him by her family, and defendant, yet when he complained of the said boy's conduct, insisted on his behaving, or he should be sent to the reform school, defendant became wrothy(sic) and thereafter refused to speak to plaintiff, and in a few weeks left plaintiff and his home, from which she has willfully absented herself continually, since June first, 1906.

"Plaintiff further alleges that defendant is guilty of gross neglect of duty, in that she paid no attention to plaintiff's comfort, neglected her household affairs, and persistently ran bills with merchants and others for articles for herself and family, not as necessaries, or even ordinary luxuries, but useless and expensive things, showing thereby a reckless disregard of plaintiff's interests and rights."

The petition went further to describe Charles G. Parker's real estate holdings and to declare that he had owned these for many years and that Isabel had no claim of ownership on them, whatsoever. Finally, a decree of absolute divorce from the defendant was requested, with any claim that she might make on the property be forever rejected.

Because Isabel had left the area for parts unknown, it was necessary to publish the notice of the divorce suit in a local paper. It first appeared in the September 20, 1907, issue of the Dwight (KS) Spirit and then in the two following issues. A copy of this published notice was mailed to Isabel's last known address in Chicago. Finally, on December 14, 1907, the divorce decree was signed, including the stipulations pertaining to the real estate that had been sought. Once more, Charles G. Parker was a free man.

(First published Friday, Sept. 20, 1907)

PUBLICATION NOTCIE

STATE OF KANSAS, } ss
   Morris County. }

In the District Court for said County.
C, G. Parker, Plaintiff.
      VS.
Isabel D. Parker, Defendant.

Said defendant Isabel D. Parker will take notice that she has been sued in the above named Court for absolute divorce on the grounds of gross neglect of duty and abandoment for over one year; also to quiet her claim and interest in certain real estate described in said petition, and must answer the petition filed therein by said plaintiff on or before the fourth day of November, A. D., 1907, or said petition will be taken as true, and judgment for plaintiff in said action for absolute divorce and exclusion from all claims to said real estate will be rendered accordingly.

   Attest: J. W. DRAKE,
             Clerk of said Court.
(SEAL)   JOHN MALOY,
  3 34   Attorney for Plaintiff.

The published notice from the Dwight (KS) Spirit

Chapter 29
The End Of The Trail

    Charles G. Parker still needed someone to care for his home and for him. At the risk of sheer speculation, it is possible that when he was in Kansas City with his cattle in the fall of 1906, he made inquiry of friends, or perhaps placed a want ad in one of the Kansas City papers. However it may have come about, at some point, he hired a young lady by the name of Rose Rennolds as his housekeeper.

    Virtually all of the information that we have about her comes from the 1910 Federal census that was enumerated by Abner Dilley on April 15, 1910. In that census, we learn that she was a widowed white female, 36 years of age, and the mother of one child who was not living with her. We also learn that she was born in Missouri and could both read and write. The last set of facts have a direct connection with her employment for Charles G. Parker. They are, first of all, she had no trade but had her own income and she owned her own home and it was free of mortgage.

    Charles G. Parker began to experience failing health late in the summer of 1909, so he knew that it was time to make some final arrangements. A last will and testament had been written up some time earlier with blanks left for the date of execution. These were filled in on the sixteenth of August, 1909. He appointed N. Dilley and Anton Goos (sometimes "Goss") as executors of his will. $50 was left to someone in Santa Fe and other amounts were left to friends and relatives in the local area. The final items are what are of interest to us. He said, "I will and bequeath to Rose Rennolds my house and household goods and all of my land situated in Section 9, of Township 15 South, Range Seven east of the 6th principal Meridian, in Morris County, Kansas, for her services and kindness to me during my life. Any residue after the foregoing named expenses and bequests have been paid, also any and all of my personal property which I may possess at my death, I will and bequeath to Rose Rennolds."[1]

    The will was signed with the hand of an old and sick Charles G. Parker and witnessed by neighbors Thomas Poole and Mary

---

[1] - Register of Deeds Office, Court House, Council Grove, KS

Dilley. The community must have heard the news that his time was short, but it didn't seem real that he might die. Probably very few of the local population could remember a time when he wasn't a resident of the area. His old body, hardened by those years on the trail, was mighty tough but he was fighting a losing battle and he passed away on September 7, 1909. The White City newspaper carried the item like this:

"Charley Parker Dead"

"The death of Chas. Parker, which occurred Tuesday, removes one of the earliest settlers in this part of the state. Mr. Parker settled at Parkerville over 40 years ago, the town deriving its name from him. He was an interesting character and very eccentric."[1]

A few days later, an unknown author wrote an obituary that appeared in the September 17th issue of the Council Grove (KS) Guard. Some details seem to conflict with what we have learned from other sources, while others add information that we have not found elsewhere. Here it is in it's entirety—

"Obituary"

"Chas. G. Parker was born in Mansfield, Windom Co., Connecticut, May 5, 1820. Died at his residence in Parkerville Tuesday, Sept. 7, '09, at 11 a.m., aged 89 years, 4 months and 2 days.

"His parents died when he was ten years old so he said "he pushed his way through life."

"He had five brothers and three sisters, all of whom preceded him to the other world several years ago. He first came to Kansas in 1849 and from that time went out in charge of a heavy government train of wagons, oxen, horses and mules and did service for nineteen years hauling freight along the old Santa Fe Trail. Sometimes, as he told the writer, having many thousands of dollars worth of goods and occasionally attacked by the Indians, but never lost any of the freight although at one time the Indians rounded up the cattle and drove them off, but Uncle Charley and a few of his men (as he had about 30 in all) saddled their horses and well armed, pursued and killed several Indians and recaptured their cattle. He told me he never lost but one man and that was because the man disobeyed his orders.

---

[1] -White City (KS) Register, September 9, 1909

"In the year of 1868 he came to Parkerville which was named for him, at which place he soon after built a large stone house which is yet in a good state of preservation and in which house he quietly passed into the beyond at the time above mentioned.

"He was a very kind hearted man, generous and hospitable. It is said by those who knew him in the early days of Kansas that "no person in need ever appealed to him for aid in vain." The beautiful park in the center of our little town stands as a monument to his memory. He told me "he had the soft maple trees" of which the park is chiefly comprised, "shipped from the south" I believe from Texas. We are informed that the deceased was elected from this county to the legislature from 1870-73.

"His was a long and hard fought battle for life. For about twenty years his health had been very bad but not until about ten days before his departure did he make up his mind that he was at the end of the race. All that could be done was done but the summons had to be obeyed. He was conscious within a few hours of his death. In earlier life, he was a member of the Presbyterian church. The funeral services were conducted by Rev. S. D. Vincent at the M. E. Church at 2 p.m. Sept. 8th and interment in the Parkerville Cemetery."

# # # # #

The executors of the estate soon set about to do their duty, with an auction scheduled for Monday, October 11, 1909. A local boy, George Dumford[1], and Jeff Cookson were hired to handle the sale, with John Drake, cashier of the newly-opened Peoples State Bank of Parkerville, serving as clerk.

We have no information about the weather on sale day, but the entire community must have gathered at the farmstead on the west side of Parkerville to see the action. About three dozen buyers vied for the assortment of farm-related items that day. One team of mules sold for $290, a gray mare brought $176, but another gray mare only brought $25. That last one was bought by Rose Rennolds. Is it

---

[1] - George Dumford had just recently graduated from auction school. He suffered the indignity of having his name misspelled in the newspaper advertisement.

possible that the horse buyers stood back and didn't bid on that one, so that Rose could have it? We'll never know.

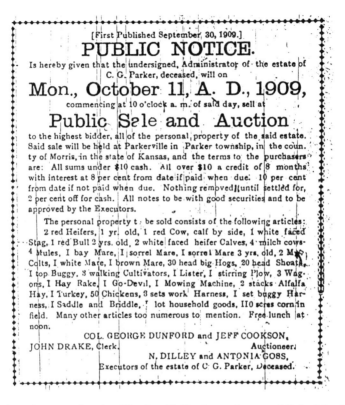

[First Published September 30, 1909.]

PUBLIC NOTICE.

Is hereby given that the undersigned, Administrator of the estate of C. G. Parker, deceased, will on

Mon., October 11, A. D., 1909,

commencing at 10 o'clock a. m. of said day, sell at

Public Sale and Auction

to the highest bidder, all of the personal, property of the said estate. Said sale will be held at Parkerville in Parker township, in the coun-ty of Morris, in the state of Kansas, and the terms to the purchasers are: All sums under $10 cash. All over $10 a credit of 8 months with interest at 8 per cent from date if paid when due. 10 per cent from date if not paid when due. Nothing removed until settled for, 2 per cent off for cash. All notes to be with good securities and to be approved by the Executors.

The personal property t be sold consists of the following articles: 2 red Heifers, 1 yr. old, 1 red Cow, calf by side, 1 white faced Stag, 1 red Bull 2 yrs. old, 2 white faced heifer Calves, 4 milch cows, 4 Mules, I bay Mare, I sorrel Mare, I sorrel Mare 3 yrs. old, 2 Mare Colts, I white Mare, I brown Mare, 30 head big Hogs, 20 head Shoats, I top Buggy, 3 walking Cultivators, I Lister, I stirring Plow, 3 Wag-ons, I Hay Rake, I Go-Devil, I Mowing Machine, 2 stacks Alfalfa Hay, I Turkey, 50 Chickens, 3 sets work Harness, I set buggy Har-ness, I Saddle and Briddle, I lot household goods, 110 acres corn in field. Many other articles too numerous to mention. Free lunch at noon.

COL. GEORGE DUNFORD and JEFF COOKSON,
JOHN DRAKE, Clerk. Auctioneers
N, DILLEY and ANTONIA GOSS,
Executors of the estate of C G. Parker, Deceased.

Advertisement for the Charles G. Parker sale as published in the Council Grove Republican, September 30, 1909.

One mowing machine brought fifty cents, but another one sold for $1.25. A sewing machine sold for fifty cents and a harrow, lister, plow and another lister altogether only brought two dollars. An incubator sold for $1.25 and a bed spring for sixty cents. On and on the small items went. Quite a number of piles of junk were sold, each bringing from twenty-five cents to two dollars.

The list of the names of the buyers is a "who's who" of the community. Among them is found J. C. Parker, Mat Baker, Ham

Rinard, Dan Easter, T. N. Haun, H. L. Burton, William Hull, I. P. Brown, Fred Seth, and George Leitch, to name a few. When the bids were all totaled up, the sale had brought in $2,316.72.

The process of settling up the estate took many month. Outstanding debts were called for and some that were submitted caused eyebrows to be raised. One such bill indicated that Charles G. Parker owed that particular individual $34.50 for "labor for putting machinery in mill in 1885."[1] "Interest on said account at 6 per cent - $49.08." The individual listed "three years service as clerk at $5 per annum - $15." Apparently, the individual was charging the estate for keeping track of his interest. He then indicated that on July 5, 1909, he had received 15 cents on the bill. Adding $4.41 more interest to the total, he concluded that the estate owed him $102.84. A notation on the bill, signed by the executors, said "We recommend that the above bill be rejected on account of statute of limitations."

The settling up of the estate was not fully completed until September 3, 1917, nearly eight years after the death of Charles G. Parker. All bills were paid, the executors were discharged, and Rose Rennolds fades from the local scene.

# # # # #

It has been one hundred and fifty years since Charles G. Parker first traveled through Council Grove on the way to Santa Fe. Perhaps not famous as some men are, still his legacy remains. If you were to drive up through the area some time in the spring and enjoy the beauty of the valley, you would understand why this was the spot he chose to call home. He called it "Parkerville."

---

[1] -Information pertaining to the estate from the archives, Clerk of the District Court, Council Grove, KS

INDEX

F

Fall, Mattie, 85
Far West, 59
Fauntleroy, Colonel Thomas, 22
Fayetteville, Arkansas, 2
Fillmore, Millard, 28
Flint Hills, 6
Fontleroy, Col. _____, 25
Fort Atkinson, 13
Fort Laramie, WY, 47
Fort Lyon, 49
Fort Marcy, 37
Fort Riley, 62
Fort Stanton, 49
Fort Sumner, 47, 48
Fritz, Capt. _____, 47

G

Gallinas Mountains, 45
Gallinas Springs, 49
Garay, Nesario, 14
Garrard, Lewis H., 11
Garrett, Pat, 47
Giddings, James, 23, 24
Gilbert, Lieutenant _____, 50
Gillet, R. H., 31
Girard, J. T., 71
Glorietta, 37
Gonzales, Mr. _____, 50
Goos, Anton, 101
Gorham, Capt. _____, 47
Gorman, John, 17, 18, 19, 31
Gregg, Josiah, 7
Griego, Francisco, 14, 17, 31, 38, 39, 40

H

Hamner, Chas., 90
Harman, P., 72
Harvey, Dr. W. T., 92, 94
Hatch, Alexander, 21, 22, 23
Haun, T. N., 105
Haun, W. H., 59

Hays, S. M., 7
Hersam, Mr. _____, 64
Hertzog, Peter, 33
Hickman, _____, 25
Holliday, Cyrus K., 52
Hopkins, Anna Lindsey, 89
Hopkins, James A., 2, 86, 89
Houghton, _____, 23
Houghton, Jacob, 31
Houghton, Judge James, 24
Huffaker, T. S., 61
Hughs, A. J., 61
Hull, William, 105

I

Independence, 6, 13
Ingram, Clara, 67
Irvin, Rev. George A., 85

J

Jackson, Capt. _____, 25
Jackson, Col. A. M., 37
Jackson, Hon. A. M., 30
James, C. N., 8
Jeffries & Sons, 26
Johnson, Clara, 60
Johnson, Elder Ezra, 74, 89
Johnson, James L., 13, 15, 17, 28, 29, 30, 31, 32
Junction City, KS, 63

K

Kansas City, 2, 8, 13, 27, 96
Kansas Press, 7, 8, 25, 27
Kaw Indian, 42
Kearny, General Stephen W., 16
Kelly, Peter, 25
Kendall, _____, 74
Kingsbury, John, 22, 26, 53
Kinner, B., 86
Kiowa Indians, 13, 17, 28
Kitchen, _____, 25

108

L

La Fonda, 33
Ladrick & Robbins, 52
Lamy, John B., 19
Las Vegas, New Mexico, 27
Lawrence, Kansas, 2
Loring, J., 32
Lovell, _____, 45

M

M.K. & T. Railroad, 62
Magoffin, Samuel, 10
Magoffin, Susan, 10
Majors & Russel, 25
Maloy, John, 92, 93, 98
Manchester County, CT, 9
Mansfield, CT, 9, 102
Marcos de Niza, 16
Marshall, John, 5
Maximilian I, 45
Maxwell, Lucian, 47
McCabe, Captain _____, 49, 51
McCollom, W. A., 61
McCray, David O., 84
McCutchen, _____, 25
McCutchen, T. K., 25
McGeorge, W. R., 90
McKenzie, Lewis, 61, 62
Medicine Lodge, KS, 47
Meggs County, Ohio, 1
Mercure, Henry, 26
Mescalero Apaches, 45, 48
Miller, A. N., 73
Milligan, _____, 25
Missouri River, 9
Moore, Judge O. L., 93
Moore, Mrs. Priscilla, 59
Morris County, 1
Morris, Captain _____, 25

N

Napoleon Bonaparte, 45
Napoleon III, 45

Neosho River, 1, 6, 7, 53, 55
New Mexico, 6
Newhold, Lieut. _____, 47
Nichols, Mr. _____, 68
Noggle, Jos., 86

O

Olney, Mr. _____, 64
Osage Indians, 6
Otero, Miguel A., 28
Owens, Richard, 17

P

Parker, Bill, 47, 56, 59
Parker, Charles and Anna, 9
Parker, Charles G., 3, 4, 6, 7, 9, 11,
    12, 13, 20, 21, 22, 23, 24, 25, 26,
    27, 29, 30, 31, 32, 33, 34, 36, 37,
    38, 39, 40, 41, 42, 43, 45, 46, 50,
    51, 52, 53, 54, 55, 56, 57, 58, 59,
    60, 61, 62, 63, 65, 70, 73, 74, 75,
    76, 77, 78, 79, 82, 83, 84, 85, 87,
    88, 91, 92, 93, 94, 95, 96, 98,
    100, 101, 104, 105
Parker, Charlottie, 59, 74, 76, 77,
    78
Parker, Drury, 59
Parker, Frank, 59, 80
Parker, Henry, 70
Parker, Henry S., 9
Parker, Isabel, 94, 95, 98, 100
Parker, J. C., 104
Parker, Mary, 70
Parker, Mattie, 3, 89, 91, 94
Parker, Miss Jessie, 90
Parkerville, 1, 2, 3, 4, 9, 68, 103
Peshamo, 14
Phillips, C. T., 92
Pierce, Franklin, 28
Pitsenburger, Sheriff _____, 95
Polk, James K., 16
Poole, Thomas, 3, 101
Porter, Mrs. _____, 67
Porter, Peter, 25

If you enjoyed "CHARLES G. PARKER; Wagonmaster On The Trail To Santa Fe," and would like to share it with friends or family, additional copies may be ordered directly from the publisher. Send $12.95 plus $2.25 shipping and handling to --

Village Press

407 Main - Parkerville St.

White City, KS 66872-9303

Kansas customers please add 76 cents Kansas sales tax.

Book retailers - for wholesale pricing, please contact us at the above address.